Standard Grade | General | Credit

German

General Level 1999
General Level Reading 1999
General Level Listening Transcript 1999
General Level Listening 1999

General Level 2000
General Level Reading 2000
General Level Listening Transcript 2000
General Level Listening 2000

General Level 2001
General Level Reading 2001
General Level Listening Transcript 2001
General Level Listening 2001

General Level 2002
General Level Reading 2002
General Level Listening Transcript 2002
General Level Listening 2002

General Level 2003
General Level Reading 2003
General Level Listening Transcript 2003
General Level Listening 2003

Credit Level 1999
Credit Level Reading 1999
Credit Level Listening Transcript 1999
Credit Level Listening 1999

Credit Level 2000
Credit Level Reading 2000
Credit Level Listening Transcript 2000
Credit Level Listening 2000

Credit Level 2001
Credit Level Reading 2001
Credit Level Listening Transcript 2001
Credit Level Listening 2001

Credit Level 2002
Credit Level Reading 2002
Credit Level Listening Transcript 2002
Credit Level Listening 2002

Credit Level 2003
Credit Level Reading 2003
Credit Level Listening Transcript 2003
Credit Level Listening 2003

Leckie × Leckie
Scotland's leading educational publishers

© Scottish Qualifications Authority

All rights reserved. Copying prohibited. No part of this publication may be reproduced, stored in a retrieval system, or transmitted in any form or by any means, electronic, mechanical, photocopying, recording or otherwise.

First exam published in 1999.
Published by
Leckie & Leckie, 8 Whitehill Terrace, St. Andrews, Scotland KY16 8RN
tel: 01334 475656 fax: 01334 477392
enquiries@leckieandleckie.co.uk www.leckieandleckie.co.uk

Leckie & Leckie Project Team: Peter Dennis; John MacPherson; Bruce Ryan; Andrea Smith
ISBN 1-84372-096-5
A CIP Catalogue record for this book is available from the British Library.
Printed in Scotland by Scotprint.
Leckie & Leckie is a division of Granada Learning Limited, part of Granada plc.

Introduction

Dear Student,

This past paper book offers you the perfect opportunity to put into practice what you should know in order to do well in your exams. As these questions have actually appeared in the exam in previous years, you can be sure they reflect the kind of questions you will be asked this summer.

Work carefully through the papers, not only to test your knowledge and understanding but also your ability to handle information and work through more thought-provoking questions. Use the answer booklet at the back of the book to check that you know exactly what the examiner is looking for to gain top marks. You will be able to focus on areas of weakness to sharpen your grasp of the subject and our top tips for revision and sitting the exam will also help to improve your performance on the day.

Remember, practice makes perfect! These past papers will show you what to expect in your exam, help to boost your confidence and feel ready to gain the grade you really want.

Good luck!

Acknowledgements

Every effort has been made to trace the copyright holders and to obtain their permission for the use of copyright material. Leckie & Leckie will gladly receive information enabling them to rectify any error or omission in subsequent editions.

1999 GENERAL

Official SQA Past Papers: General German 1999

FOR OFFICIAL USE

Presenting Centre No.	Subject No.	Level	Paper No.	Group No.	Marker's No.
	1300				

G

Total

1300/102

SCOTTISH
CERTIFICATE OF
EDUCATION
1999

WEDNESDAY, 26 MAY
G/C   9.20 AM – 10.05 AM
F/G   10.05 AM – 10.50 AM

**GERMAN
STANDARD GRADE**
General Level
Reading

Fill in these boxes and read what is printed below.

Full name of school or college

Town

First name and initials

Surname

Date of birth
Day Month Year

Candidate number

Number of seat

When you are told to do so, open your paper and write your answers **in English** in the spaces provided.

You may use a German dictionary.

Before leaving the examination room you must give this book to the invigilator. If you do not, you may lose all the marks for this paper.

SCOTTISH
QUALIFICATIONS
AUTHORITY

MCB 1300/102 6/19920

Your German pen friend has sent you her local newspaper and some magazines.

1. A local girl, Katrin Wypior, is "Young Personality of the Week" in the newspaper.

Ich bin fünfzehn und spiele seit fünf Jahren Geige.

Mein Haupthobby ist aber Schwimmen. Klassische Musik höre ich nie. Ich höre lieber Gruppen wie 911.

Mein Traum ist es, eine Weltreise zu machen.

Mein größter Fehler ist wahrscheinlich, daß ich sehr faul bin. Was ich an mir besonders mag: ich komme prima mit meinen Freunden aus.

Katrin Wypior

Complete the grid. (4)

Name	**Katrin Wypior**
Age	15
Main hobby	Swimming
Favourite music	Groups like 911
Her dream	
Worst fault	
Best quality	

2. There are some adverts for sports shops in the newspaper.

A

Achtung Sportler!
Große Auswahl an Sportbekleidung und Schuhen

Mo. – Fr.   9.00 – 17.00 Uhr
Sa.   9.00 – 13.00 Uhr
So.   geschlossen

B

Freizeitwelt

Boote, Bootsmotoren, Wassersport, Camping, Zelte, Propangas

(So. geschlossen)

C

kleine freizeit ...   **Ihr Sportschuhgeschäft**

Wir haben geöffnet:

Mo., Di., Do., Fr. 9.00 – 23.00 Uhr
Mi. 6.00 – 23.00 Uhr
Sa., So. 10.00 – 18.00 Uhr

	Letter
Where could you buy a track suit?	
Which shop is open every day?	

(2)

3. You see an advert for a trip to Scotland.

Die Schottland-&-History-&-Mystery-Tour

1. Tag	Aus Hamburg kommen Sie um 15.30 Uhr in Newcastle an. Sie fahren dann direkt zur schottischen Hauptstadt, wo Sie übernachten.
3. Tag	Tageswanderung (6–8 Stunden) durch das schottische Hochland. Abendessen in einem schönen, alten Schloß.
5. Tag	Sie haben die Möglichkeit, in Inverness einen Einkaufsbummel zu machen. Nachmittags besichtigen Sie einen schottischen Garten.

What do you do on these days? Write **two** things for each day. **(6)**

Day 1	
Day 3	
Day 5	

4. In a magazine you find some ideas for different kinds of parties.

Mafia Party

Klamotten: Schwarzer Hut und Sonnenbrille.
Essen und Getränke: Italienisch mit Rotwein.
Action: Mit Wasserpistolen schießen.

Urlaubsparty

Klamotten: Kurze Hose und Hawaiihemd.
Essen und Getränke: Grillen und Limo.
Action: Fahrradtour zum Strand.

Choose any **one** of the parties and say what it would be like. (3)

What would you wear at this party?	
What would you eat and drink?	
What would you do?	

5. These young people write what they think about holidays.
Constanze and Franz find holidays boring.

Constanze: Ich finde Ferien langweilig. Denn ich bin oft allein zu Hause. Außerdem gehe ich gerne zur Schule. Da ist immer was los.

Franz: Ich finde Ferien langweilig. Meine Eltern sind tagsüber an der Arbeit, und ich muß immer im Haushalt helfen, abspülen, Essen vorbereiten . . .

(a) Why do Constanze and Franz find holidays boring? Write **one** thing for each person. (2)

Constanze	
Franz	

Sebastian and Nicola enjoy their holidays.

Sebastian: Ferien sind doch einfach super! Wir fahren als Familie immer nach Spanien. Dort bin ich von früh bis spät mit meinen spanischen Freunden.

Nicola: Ferien sind fast das Schönste im ganzen Jahr! Ich kann mich ausschlafen und tun, wozu ich Lust habe.

(b) Why do they enjoy their holidays? Write **one** thing for each person. (2)

| Sebastian | |
| Nicola | |

[Turn over

6. This article gives you three exercises for your legs.

Tun Sie mehr für Ihre Beine.

Übung A Legen Sie sich auf den Rücken, strecken Sie die Beine in die Luft und bewegen Sie die Beine, wie beim Fahrradfahren.

Übung B Sie legen sich auf den Rücken. Heben Sie die Beine gestreckt etwa zwanzig Zentimeter über den Boden und halten sie so für ein paar Sekunden ruhig in der Luft. Sie legen sie wieder ab und wiederholen die Übung 10 mal.

Übung C Sie stellen sich barfuß auf die Zehenspitzen und wieder zurück. Nach 10 bis 20 Zehenständen schütteln Sie die Beine aus.

Match the pictures to the instructions. Write the correct letter in each box. (2)

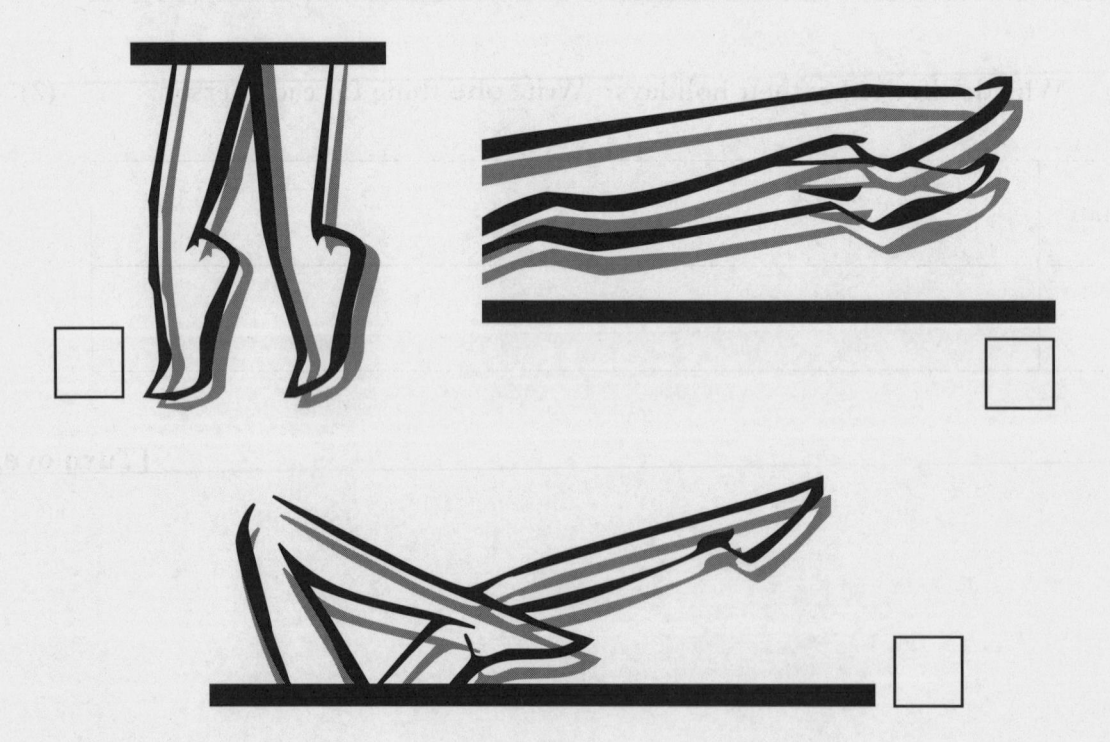

7. This article is about a phone card Germans can use when on holiday abroad.

.T. . .Card .

Mit der T-Card Holiday von der Deutschen Telekom können Sie in fünfundsechzig Ländern von fast jedem Telefon aus telefonieren.

Die Karte kann man aber auch in Deutschland benutzen.

Die T-Card Holiday gibt's für 25 oder 50 DM, und ist bei der Post zu kaufen.

Only **three** of the following statements are true. Tick (✓) the three statements which are true.

(3)

	Tick (✓)
You can use the card in 65 countries.	
You can use it for any telephone.	
You can also use it in Germany.	
You cannot use it in Germany.	
You can buy it at the post office.	

[Turn over

8. These young people say what their idea of beauty is.

Was ist „schön"?

Thomas:	Wie man aussieht, ist nicht so wichtig. Hauptsache, man ist sympathisch, freundlich und hilfsbereit.
Andrea:	Ich trage jeden Tag Make-up und ziehe mich schick an. So bin ich immer guter Laune.
Klaus:	Es ist mir gleich, wie ich aussehe. Man muß mich einfach nehmen, wie ich bin.
Peter:	Ich mag Mädchen mit blonden, kurzen Haaren. Lockiges, rotes Haar finde ich schrecklich.
Wibke:	Leute, die glücklich sind, sind natürlich schön.

Who say the following things? Write the correct name in each box. **(4)**

	Name
People must take me the way I am.	
Happy people are beautiful people.	
It's more important to **be** nice than to **look** nice.	
It makes me feel better if I try to look good.	
Hair style and colour are important.	

9. A boy describes a sailing trip with his father from America to the Canary Islands.

ABENTEUER AUF SEE

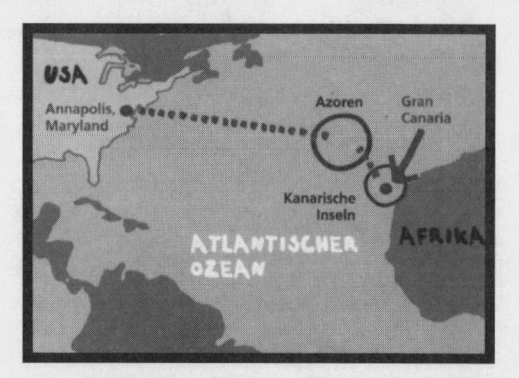

Am dritten Tag rief mein Vater plötzlich, „Sieh mal, ein Wal!" Fünfmal insgesamt kam der Wal aus dem Wasser und atmete schwer. „Gut 15 Meter ist er lang," meinte mein Vater. Der Wal schwamm direkt vor unserem Boot.
Das Schlimmste und Schrecklichste auf der Reise war der Sturm. Am Mittwoch, als ich erwachte, war es acht Uhr morgens. Der Wind heulte fürchterlich. Mitte des nächsten Tages ließ der Sturm nach.

(a) One day they saw a whale. What did it do? Write **two** things. (2)

(b) What was the whale like? Write **one** thing. (1)

(c) When did the storm die down? (1)

Total (32)

[END OF QUESTION PAPER]

[BLANK PAGE]

1300/107

SCOTTISH
CERTIFICATE OF
EDUCATION
1999

WEDNESDAY, 26 MAY
11.55 AM – 12.20 PM
(APPROX)

**GERMAN
STANDARD GRADE**
General Level
Listening Transcript

This paper must not be seen by any candidate.

The material overleaf is provided for use in an emergency only (eg the tape or equipment proving faulty) or where permission has been given in advance by SQA for the material to be read to candidates with special needs. The material must be read exactly as printed.

Transcript—General Level

> **Instructions to reader(s):**
>
> For each item, read the English **once**, then read the German **twice**, with an interval of 7 seconds between the two readings. On completion of the second reading, pause for the length of time indicated in brackets after each item, to allow the candidates to write their answers.
>
> Where special arrangements have been agreed in advance to allow the reading of the material, those sections marked **(f)** should be read by a female speaker and those marked **(m)** by a male: those sections marked **(t)** should be read by the teacher.

(t) You are staying with a German family in Friedrichsstadt, a small town in North Germany.

(f) or (m) **Du wohnst bei einer deutschen Familie in Friedrichsstadt, einer Kleinstadt in Norddeutschland.**

(t) Question number one.

Your pen friend, Jörg, has arranged for you to visit his school.

When do you have to be at school tomorrow?

(m) **Ich habe organisiert, daß du morgen mit mir in die Schule kommst. Wir müssen um Viertel vor acht da sein.**

(30 seconds)

(t) Question number two.

What subject does Jörg have Period 3 tomorrow?

(m) **Ich habe morgen eine Doppelstunde Englisch, und dann in der dritten Stunde Mathe.**

(30 seconds)

(t) Question number three.

Jörg explains how you will get to school.

Tick **three** boxes to show how you will get there.

(m) **Zuerst fahren wir mit dem Rad zum Bahnhof. Dann geht's mit dem Zug weiter. Die Schule ist dann nur fünf Minuten zu Fuß entfernt.**

(30 seconds)

(t) Question number four.

Jörg suggests what you could do in the afternoon.

What does he suggest? Tick **two** boxes.

(m) **Morgen nachmittag habe ich von 14 bis 15.30 Uhr Handball. Wenn du Lust hast, kannst du mitkommen und sehen, wie wir Handball spielen. Oder du könntest dir den Hafen ansehen.**

(30 seconds)

[1300/107] *Page two*

Official SQA Past Papers: General German 1999

(t) Question number five.

In the morning, Jörg's mother prepares a packed lunch for you.

What does she give you to drink?

(f) Ich habe euch Brötchen geschmiert. Dazu habe ich Joghurt, einen Apfel und zwei Tüten Orangensaft eingepackt. Vergeßt nicht, alles mitzunehmen!

(30 seconds)

(t) Question number six.

After you get home from school, Jörg tells you what he must do that evening.

What must he do?

What is he preparing for?

(m) Heute Abend muß ich für eine Stunde zu meiner Musikgruppe in die Stadthalle. Wir üben für ein Konzert, das wir Weihnachten geben.

(30 seconds)

(t) Question number seven.

Jörg's mother tells you what her other three children do.

Draw a line from each person to show what they do.

(f) Jörgs Schwester, Inge, ist in Kiel auf der Uni. Sie studiert Tiermedizin. Sein Bruder, Friedel, ist Apotheker in Hamburg, und die kleine Petra geht noch in die Grundschule.

(30 seconds)

(t) Question number eight.

Jörg's father tells you about his work.

What does he do?

(m) Ich bin Ingenieur auf der MS Hamburg. Das ist eine große Fähre, die dreimal in der Woche zwischen Hamburg und England fährt.

(30 seconds)

(t) Question number nine.

How often does Jörg's father have to work?

(m) Ich habe jede zweite Woche frei und kann also die Zeit hier zu Hause verbringen. Diese Woche habe ich frei und nächste Woche muß ich wieder arbeiten.

(30 seconds)

[Turn over for Questions 10 to 14 on *Page four*

Official SQA Past Papers: General German 1999

(t) **Question number ten.**

Jörg's mother suggests what you could all do on Saturday.

What does she suggest doing?

(f) **Mein Mann muß Samstag am frühen Morgen wieder nach Hamburg zum Schiff. Wir könnten alle nach Hamburg fahren. Wir könnten an Bord zu Mittag essen und nachmittags mit der U-Bahn in die Stadtmitte fahren.**

(30 seconds)

(t) **Question number eleven.**

Jörg suggests what you could do on Saturday night.

What does he suggest? Write **two** things.

(m) **Ja, das ist eine tolle Idee. Wir könnten dann am Samstagabend ins Kino gehen. Nachher könnten wir alle bei meinem Bruder Friedel übernachten.**

(30 seconds)

(t) **Question number twelve.**

Jörg's mother says she will phone his brother Friedel. You hear the conversation.

What do you hear her say? Tick **two** boxes.

(f) **Hallo Friedel! Morgen kommen wir alle nach Hamburg. Wir werden Samstag Abend gegen 19.00 Uhr bei dir ankommen.**

(30 seconds)

(t) **Question number thirteen.**

Jörg's mother tells you what Friedel has said on the phone.

What will you do with Friedel on Sunday morning? Write **one** thing.

(f) **Friedel hat euch am Sonntagvormittag zum Schlittschuhlaufen eingeladen. Das Eisstadion ist nicht weit von seiner Wohnung.**

(30 seconds)

(t) **Question number fourteen.**

What will you do with Friedel in the afternoon? Write **three** things.

(f) **Am Nachmittag macht ihr einen kleinen Sonntagsspaziergang. Friedel will euch ein bißchen von der Stadt zeigen. Gegen vier Uhr gibt's dann Kaffee und Kuchen bei Friedel.**

(30 seconds)

(t) **End of test.**

You now have 5 minutes to look over your answers.

[END OF TRANSCRIPT]

Official SQA Past Papers: General German 1999

FOR OFFICIAL USE

Presenting Centre No.	Subject No.	Level	Paper No.	Group No.	Marker's No.
	1300				

G

Total Mark

1300/106

SCOTTISH
CERTIFICATE OF
EDUCATION
1999

WEDNESDAY, 26 MAY
11.55 AM – 12.20 PM
(APPROX)

**GERMAN
STANDARD GRADE**
General Level
Listening

Fill in these boxes and read what is printed below.

Full name of school or college

Town

First name and initials

Surname

Date of birth
Day Month Year   Candidate number   Number of seat

When you are told to do so, open your paper.

You will hear a number of short items in German. You will hear each item twice, then you will have time to write your answer.

Write your answers, **in English**, in this book, in the appropriate spaces.

You may take notes as you are listening to the German, but only in this paper.

You may **not** use a German dictionary.

You are not allowed to leave the examination room until the end of the test.

Before leaving the examination room you must give this book to the invigilator. If you do not, you may lose all the marks for this paper.

SCOTTISH
QUALIFICATIONS
AUTHORITY

You are staying with a German family in Friedrichsstadt, a small town in North Germany.

Du wohnst bei einer deutschen Familie in Friedrichsstadt, einer Kleinstadt in Norddeutschland.

1. Your pen friend, Jörg, has arranged for you to visit his school.

   When do you have to be at school tomorrow? (1)

   _____

   * * * * *

2. What subject does Jörg have Period 3 tomorrow? (1)

   _____

   * * * * *

3. Jörg explains how you will get to school.

   Tick (✓) **three** boxes to show how you will get there. (3)

	Tick (✓)
Bike	
Bus	
Car	
Train	
Tram	
On foot	

   * * * * *

4. Jörg suggests what you could do in the afternoon.

What does he suggest? Tick (✓) **two** boxes. (2)

	Tick (✓)
Watch him playing handball	
Watch handball on TV	
Go on a boat trip	
Visit harbour	
Go shopping	

* * * * *

5. In the morning, Jörg's mother prepares a packed lunch for you.

What does she give you to drink? (1)

_____

* * * * *

6. After you get home from school, Jörg tells you what he must do that evening.

(*a*) What must he do? (1)

_____

(*b*) What is he preparing for? (1)

_____

* * * * *

[Turn over

7. Jörg's mother tells you what her other three children do.
Draw a line from each person to show what they do. (3)

Inge

Friedel

Petra

| bank clerk |
| teacher |
| school pupil |
| chemist |
| doctor |
| student |

* * * * *

8. Jörg's father tells you about his work.

What does he do? (1)

_____

* * * * *

9. How often does Jörg's father have to work? (1)

_____

* * * * *

10. Jörg's mother suggests what you could all do on Saturday.

What does she suggest doing? (3)

Saturday morning	
Saturday lunchtime	
Saturday afternoon	

* * * * *

11. Jörg suggests what you could do on Saturday night.

What does he suggest? Write **two** things. (2)

_____

_____

* * * * *

12. Jörg's mother says she will phone his brother Friedel. You hear the conversation.

What do you hear her say? Tick (✓) **two** boxes. (2)

- WE'RE ALL COMING TO HAMBURG TOMORROW. ☐
- WILL YOU BE IN HAMBURG TOMORROW? ☐
- WE WILL ARRIVE ON SATURDAY. ☐
- WE WILL ARRIVE ON SUNDAY. ☐

* * * * *

13. Jörg's mother tells you what Friedel has said on the phone.

What will you do with Friedel on Sunday morning? Write **one** thing. (1)

_____

* * * * *

[Turn over for Question 14 on *Page six*

14. What will you do with Friedel in the afternoon? Write **three** things. (3)

_____

_____

_____

* * * * *

Total (26)

[END OF QUESTION PAPER]

2000 GENERAL

Official SQA Past Papers: General German 2000

FOR OFFICIAL USE

G

Total

1300/402

NATIONAL QUALIFICATIONS 2000

WEDNESDAY, 7 JUNE
G/C 9.20 AM – 10.05 AM
F/G 10.05 AM – 10.50 AM

GERMAN STANDARD GRADE
General Level
Reading

Fill in these boxes and read what is printed below.

Full name of centre

Town

Forename(s)

Surname

Date of birth
Day Month Year

Scottish candidate number

Number of seat

When you are told to do so, open your paper and write your answers **in English** in the spaces provided.

You may use a German dictionary.

Before leaving the examination room you must give this book to the invigilator. If you do not, you may lose all the marks for this paper.

SCOTTISH QUALIFICATIONS AUTHORITY

MCB 1300/402 6/20120

Your German pen friend has sent you a magazine to read.

1. A boy writes about his dog.

Mein Hund

Mein Hund ist ein Dackel. Er ist nicht sehr groß und ist sehr intelligent. Am liebsten mag ich ihn, weil er so freundlich ist.

What does he like **best** about his dog? Tick (✓) the correct box.

	Tick (✓)
It is small.	
It is very clever.	
It is friendly.	

2. These young people write about holiday jobs they have done.

Sven
Ich habe einmal in den Ferien für einen Freund Zeitungen ausgetragen. Für nur drei Stunden die Woche habe ich 50DM verdient. Das war ganz prima.

Daniel
Mein bester Ferienjob war als Eisverkäufer am Strand. Ich bin in der Sonne schön braun geworden.

Anne
Letztes Jahr habe ich für eine Nachbarfamilie gearbeitet. Ich mußte auf die Kinder aufpassen und mit der Hausarbeit helfen. Das habe ich aber gern gemacht, weil ich Kinder sehr mag.

(a) What jobs did these young people do?

(b) What did they like about their jobs?

6

Sven	Job: _____ Why he liked it: _____
Daniel	Job: _____ Why he liked it: _____
Anne	Job (Write **two** things): _____ Why she liked it: _____

3. This article is about the girl on the front cover of the magazine.

> Ich heiße Anne-Marie, bin sechzehn Jahre alt und komme aus Bremen.
>
> In meiner Freizeit spiele ich Fußball und segle gern mit meinem Freund. Ich lese gern.
>
> Ich hasse Leute, die mit offenem Mund essen.

Complete the grid.

4

Name	Anne-Marie
Age	16
Interests/Hobbies **Write three things.**	
Dislikes	

4. You see an advert for a zoo. The map shows you how to get there.

> Fahr auf der A5 Richtung Kassel. Du nimmst die zweite Straße links und dann die erste rechts. Nach einem Kilometer fährst du wieder links. Der Zooeingang ist auf der linken Seite.

Mark the zoo on the map. Tick (✓) the correct box.

5. You read a long-range weather forecast for the month of August.

Bis zur Mitte des Monats bleibt das sommerliche Wetter mit viel Sonnenschein und hohen Temperaturen wie im Juli.

In der zweiten Hälfte des Monats ändert sich das Wetter. Das Thermometer sinkt um drei bis fünf Grad und am Ende des Monats gibt es ziemlich viel Regen.

What will the weather be like?

First half of August? (Write **two** things.)	
Second half of August? (Write **two** things.)	

6. Your uncle is going to have a holiday in Germany. You show him this advert from your magazine.

Hotel zum Sänger

Tick (✓)

* Freizeitzentrum und Schwimmbad im Hotel ☐

* Viele Haustiere für unsere Gästekinder ☐

* Saubere und moderne Gästezimmer ☐

* Gutes Restaurant mit Blick auf die Berge ☐

* Nur 800m von der Stadtmitte ☐

* Schöne, ruhige Lage ☐

Your uncle wants a hotel with:

* sports facilities
* good, clean rooms
* quiet location

Tick **three** of the boxes above to show that the hotel has what he is looking for.

3

[Turn over

7. These young people write about their wishes.

Markus: Die Erwachsenen sollen mir zuhören, wenn ich Probleme habe.

Steffi: Ich wünsche mir, daß alle Kinder ohne Angst vor Bomben leben können.

Elmar: Ich möchte eine bessere Arbeitsstelle finden, weil ich meine Arbeit in der Fabrik stinklangweilig finde.

Inge: Ich möchte, daß die Schule später anfängt und daß wir längere Ferien haben.

7. (continued)

What do they wish? Write **one** thing for each person.

Markus _____

Steffi _____

Elmar _____

Inge _____

[Turn over

8. You see an advert for a special kind of T-shirt.

> In der Stadtmitte siehst du einen Jungen. Du möchtest ihn kennenlernen. Aber wie?
>
> Zum Glück trägt er ein 'E-shirt.' Da steht seine E-mail Adresse gleich hinten drauf, und du kannst ihn einfach anmailen. Das E-shirt bekommst du für 39,90 Mark über die Web-site www.adresse.de.

Complete these sentences:

(a) The T-shirt is special because it has _____ on it. **1**

(b) You can buy it for 39.90 Marks from _____ . **1**

9. This article is about how to help the environment.

1. Kochst du Wasser, dann leg immer einen Deckel auf den Topf. Das Wasser kocht schneller und du sparst Energie.

2. Energiesparen in deinem Zimmer: laß nie eine Lampe brennen. Dreh die Heizung zurück, ein Pullover wärmt auch!

3. Achte darauf, daß auch in deiner Familie Müll getrennt wird. Bring selbst jede Woche das Altglas zum Container.

4. Geh zu Fuß oder nimm das Fahrrad, wenn du kurze Strecken hast. Nur im Notfall bitte die Eltern, dich mit dem Auto hinzufahren.

Match the words with the pictures. Write the correct number in each box.

Picture	Number
A	
B	
C	
D	

[Turn over for Question 10 on *Page twelve*

10. This article gives you some tips about how to be happy.

Super-Happy!

5 Tips für gute Laune!

A. Neue Pläne sind ein guter Weg aus einem Tief. Schreib 10 Sachen auf, die du machen willst!

B. Neue Klamotten und eine andere Frisur wirken Wunder.

C. Wenn du gut und viel schläfst, fühlst du dich viel besser.

D. Setz dich ruhig in eine Ecke und lies mal ein gutes Buch oder hör dir eine CD an!

E. Mit dem Rad statt mit dem Bus zur Schule fahren.

Match the tips to the headings below. Write the correct letter in each box.

	Letter
Keep fit.	
Get enough sleep.	
Make resolutions.	
Do some reading and relaxing.	
Change your appearance.	

Total (32)

[END OF QUESTION PAPER]

1300/407

NATIONAL QUALIFICATIONS 2000

WEDNESDAY, 7 JUNE 11.55 AM – 12.20 PM (APPROX)

GERMAN STANDARD GRADE
General Level
Listening Transcript

This paper must not be seen by any candidate.

The material overleaf is provided for use in an emergency only (eg the tape or equipment proving faulty) or where permission has been given in advance by SQA for the material to be read to candidates with special needs. The material must be read exactly as printed.

Transcript—General Level

> **Instructions to reader(s):**
> For each item, read the English **once,** then read the German **three times**, with an interval of 5 seconds between the readings. On completion of the third reading, pause for the length of time indicated in brackets after each item, to allow the candidates to write their answers.
>
> Where special arrangements have been agreed in advance to allow the reading of the material, those sections marked **(f)** should be read by a female speaker and those marked **(m)** by a male: those sections marked **(t)** should be read by the teacher.

(t) You are youth hostelling in Germany.

(f) or (m)   Du bist auf Urlaub in Deutschland. Du übernachtest in Jugendherbergen.

(t) Question number one.

You arrive at a hostel. The warden speaks to you.

Do you get a single room? When is breakfast? Tick the correct boxes.

(f) or (m)   Guten Tag! Also, du hast ein Zimmer zusammen mit drei anderen. Es gibt um halb acht Frühstück.

(30 seconds)

(t) Question number two.

You get to know a boy called Dieter. He invites you to join him for the day.

What does he want to do in town? Tick **two** boxes.

(m)   Hast du Lust, mit in die Stadt zu gehen? Zuerst muß ich zur Post - ich brauche Briefmarken. Ich gehe später ins Automobilmuseum. Dort gibt es tolle Autos.

(30 seconds)

(t) Question number three.

You are in town with Dieter. You go to a restaurant for lunch.

What does Dieter order? Tick the **three** correct items on the menu.

(m)   Das Essen hier ist immer sehr gut. Ich glaube, ich nehme die Tomatensuppe und . . . das Hähnchen mit Salzkartoffeln. Als Nachtisch nehme ich den Eisbecher!

(30 seconds)

(t) Question number four.

In the restaurant, Dieter shows you a picture of his family.

Which of these people is his younger sister? Put a tick at the correct person.

(m)   Das ist meine Familie. Die hier rechts ist meine ältere Schwester, Monika. Das hier ist meine Kusine, Barbara. Ganz links ist meine jüngere Schwester, Christine.

(30 seconds)

(t) **Question number five.**

Dieter asks you about where you live.

What does he want to know? Tick **two** things.

(m) **Wie groß ist deine Stadt? Ich meine, wie viele leben dort? Wohnst du in einem Haus mit Garten oder in einer Wohnung?**

(30 seconds)

(t) **Question number six.**

Dieter invites you to go on a coach trip the next day to see something of the area.

Where does the trip leave from?

(m) **Also, morgen machen wir einen Ausflug mit dem Bus. Abfahrt ist am Marktplatz.**

(30 seconds)

(t) **Question number seven.**

He explains what you will do on the trip.

What will you do in the morning and in the afternoon?

(m) **Am Morgen besuchen wir ein herrliches altes Schloß. Da hat unser König Ludwig gelebt. Am Nachmittag machen wir eine Bootsfahrt auf dem See.**

(30 seconds)

(t) **Question number eight.**

At the youth hostel, you meet a girl called Sandra. She says she will be playing at a concert tomorrow in the town hall.

What else does she tell you about herself? Write **two** things.

(f) **Ich komme aus Bern in der Schweiz. Ich bin mit meinem Schulorchester hier. Morgen geben wir ein Konzert. Ich spiele Klavier.**

(30 seconds)

(t) **Question number nine.**

Sandra gives you a ticket for the concert. She tells you how to get there.

How can you get there? Tick **two** of the boxes.

(f) **Du fährst mit der Straßenbahn, Linie 8, bis zum Stadion. Oder du kannst auch zu Fuß hingehen, wenn du Lust hast.**

(30 seconds)

[Turn over for Questions 10 to 14 on *Page four*

(t) Question number ten.

She gives you directions from the stadium to the hall where they are playing.

Put a cross on the plan to show where the hall is.

(f) Vom Stadion gehst du geradeaus. Du nimmst die zweite Straße links. Die Halle findest du dann auf der rechten Seite.

(30 seconds)

(t) Question number eleven.

You hear Sandra telling a friend on the phone what she likes and doesn't like about her stay at the youth hostel.

What does she **not** like? Tick **two** boxes.

(f) Die Leute hier sind sehr freundlich, muß ich sagen. Mein Zimmer ... mag ich nicht so sehr: Es ist ziemlich klein ... Das Essen hier schmeckt wirklich gut. Das Wetter? Du liebe Zeit! Scheußlich, es regnet jeden Tag!

(30 seconds)

(t) Question number twelve.

Sandra invites you to her parents' flat for a few days.

What does she tell you about their flat? Write **two** things.

(f) Wir haben eine Fünfzimmerwohnung. Sie liegt in der Stadtmitte. Wir haben Platz genug für dich.

(30 seconds)

(t) Question number thirteen.

She says you could also visit her grandparents.

What does she say about where they live? Write **two** things.

(f) Wir könnten auch meine Großeltern besuchen. Sie wohnen in einem kleinen Dorf in den Bergen, 50 Kilometer von Bern entfernt.

(30 seconds)

(t) Question number fourteen.

How will you get to Sandra's flat?

How long will it take to get there?

(f) Mein Vater kommt am Wochenende mit dem Auto. Wir können zusammen mit ihm nach Hause fahren. Die Reise dauert ungefähr zwei Stunden.

(30 seconds)

(t) End of test.

Now look over your answers.

[END OF TRANSCRIPT]

Official SQA Past Papers: General German 2000

FOR OFFICIAL USE

G

Total Mark

1300/406

NATIONAL QUALIFICATIONS 2000

WEDNESDAY, 7 JUNE
11.55 AM – 12.20 PM
(APPROX)

**GERMAN
STANDARD GRADE**
General Level
Listening

Fill in these boxes and read what is printed below.

Full name of centre

Town

Forename(s)

Surname

Date of birth
Day Month Year

Scottish candidate number

Number of seat

When you are told to do so, open your paper.

You will hear a number of short items in German. You will hear each item three times, then you will have time to write your answer.

Write your answers, **in English**, in this book, in the appropriate spaces.

You may take notes as you are listening to the German, but only in this paper.

You may **not** use a German dictionary.

You are not allowed to leave the examination room until the end of the test.

Before leaving the examination room you must give this book to the invigilator. If you do not, you may lose all the marks for this paper.

SCOTTISH QUALIFICATIONS AUTHORITY

MCB 1300/406 6/20120

You are youth hostelling in Germany.

Du bist auf Urlaub in Deutschland. Du übernachtest in Jugendherbergen.

1. You arrive at a hostel. The warden speaks to you. Tick (✓) the correct boxes.

   (a) Do you get a single room?   Yes [ ]   No [ ]

   (b) When is breakfast?   7.30 [ ]   8.30 [ ]

   * * * * *

2. You get to know a boy called Dieter. He invites you to join him for the day. What does he want to do in town? Tick (✓) **two** boxes.

	Tick (✓)
Buy postcards	
Buy stamps	
Go to a museum	
Hire a car	

   * * * * *

3. You are in town with Dieter. You go to a restaurant for lunch.

What does Dieter order? Tick (✓) the **three** correct items on the menu.

Mushroom soup ☐

Tomato soup ☐

Pea soup ☐

Chicken ☐

Ham ☐

Pork ☐

Apple tart ☐

Fruit salad ☐

Ice cream ☐

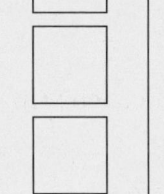

* * * * *

4. In the restaurant, Dieter shows you a picture of his family.

Which of these people is his younger sister? Put a tick (✓) at the correct person.

* * * * *

5. Dieter asks you about where you live.

What does he want to know? Tick (✓) **two** things.

He wants to know . . .

	Tick (✓)
. . . where your town is.	
. . . how many people live there.	
. . . how long you have stayed there.	
. . . the kind of house you live in.	

Marks

2

* * * * *

6. Dieter invites you to go on a coach trip the next day to see something of the area.

Where does the trip leave from?

_____

1

* * * * *

7. He explains what you will do on the trip. What will you do:

(*a*) In the morning? _____

1

(*b*) In the afternoon? _____

1

* * * * *

8. At the youth hostel, you meet a girl called Sandra. She says she will be playing at a concert tomorrow in the town hall.

What else does she tell you about herself? Write **two** things.

_____

_____

2

* * * * *

[1300/406] Page four

Marks

9. Sandra gives you a ticket for the concert. She tells you how to get there.
   How can you get there? Tick (✓) **two** of the boxes.

   2

   * * * * *

10. She gives you directions from the stadium to the hall where they are playing.
    Put a cross (✗) on the plan to show where the hall is.

    1

    Stadium

    * * * * *

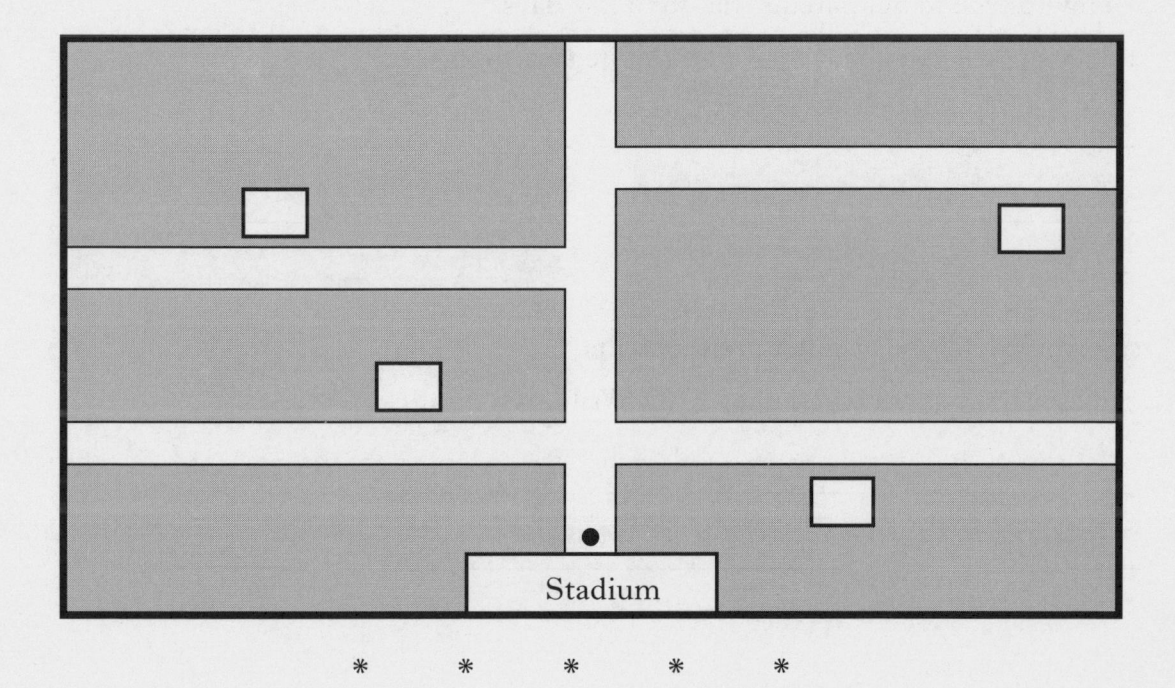

[Turn over for Questions 11 to 14 on *Page six*

[1300/406]   *Page five*

Marks

11. You hear Sandra telling a friend on the phone what she likes and doesn't like about her stay at the youth hostel.

What does she **not** like? Tick (✓) **two** boxes.   2

	Tick (✓)
The people	
Her room	
The food	
The weather	

* * * * *

12. Sandra invites you to her parents' flat for a few days.

What does she tell you about their flat? Write **two** things.   2

_____

_____

* * * * *

13. She says you could also visit her grandparents.

What does she say about where they live? Write **two** things.   2

_____

_____

* * * * *

14. (*a*) How will you get to Sandra's flat?   1

_____

(*b*) How long will it take to get there?   1

_____

* * * * *

Total (26)

[*END OF QUESTION PAPER*]

2001 GENERAL

Official SQA Past Papers: General German 2001

FOR OFFICIAL USE

Total

1300/402

NATIONAL QUALIFICATIONS 2001

WEDNESDAY, 6 JUNE
G/C 9.20 AM – 10.05 AM
F/G 10.05 AM – 10.50 AM

GERMAN STANDARD GRADE
General Level
Reading

G

Fill in these boxes and read what is printed below.

Full name of centre

Town

Forename(s)

Surname

Date of birth
Day Month Year

Scottish candidate number

Number of seat

When you are told to do so, open your paper and write your answers **in English** in the spaces provided.

You may use a German dictionary.

Before leaving the examination room you must give this book to the invigilator. If you do not, you may lose all the marks for this paper.

SCOTTISH QUALIFICATIONS AUTHORITY

MCB 1300/402 6/21520

You are staying in a hotel in Germany on holiday.

1. Your father sees this advertisement for a trip to Berlin.

Bahntour
REISEN MIT DER BAHN 1. KLASSE
20. bis 25. Juli 2001
GROSSE THEATERFAHRT

6 TAGE

Berlin

PREISE
Einzelzimmer	DM 60 pro Tag
Doppelzimmer	DM 85 pro Tag
Stadtrundfahrt	DM 55
Eintrittskarten für das Theater	DM 16
(Erwachsene)	
(Schüler und Studenten)	DM 10
Kinokarten	DM 20

(a) How do you travel to Berlin? Tick (✓) the correct box.

	Tick (✓)
Plane	
Coach	
Train	

(b) What would your father have to pay for his theatre ticket?

(c) What is the price of a double room?

2. There is a free magazine in your room. This article gives you tips about how to choose a job that will suit you.

Wie wählt man einen Beruf?

- Welche Interessen hast du?
- Was ist für dich im Leben wichtig?
- Wo hast du schon während der Schulzeit gearbeitet?
- Was sind deine Lieblingsfächer in der Schule?

What questions do you need to ask yourself?

Choose **three** questions and say what they are.

3

3. This article is about some of the people who work in a German hotel.

Wer ist wer im Hotel?

Doorman
Das ist der Herr im langen Mantel am Haupteingang. Er begrüßt die Gäste und öffnet Autotüren für sie.

Hausdame
Das ist die Frau mit der weißen Bluse und dem dunklen Rock. Man geht zur Hausdame, wenn das Telefon kaputt ist, oder wenn man die Zahnbürste vergisst.

Restaurantdirektor
Er trägt einen schwarzen Anzug oder eine weiße Jacke. Er führt die Gäste an ihren Tisch und gibt ihnen die Speisekarte.

Fill in the grid.

	What do they wear?	What do they do? Write **one** thing for each person.
Doorman	(Write **one** thing.)	
Hausdame (Hotel Housekeeper)	(Write **two** things.)	
Restaurantdirektor (Restaurant Manager)	(Write **two** things.)	

4. You look at the television programmes for this evening.

18.30 Uhr	Wer ist hier der Boss? US–Comedy–Serie.
19.00 Uhr	Länderspiel Deutschland gegen Ungarn im Handball.
20.00 Uhr	Polizeichef Bergmann untersucht den Tod eines Bankchefs—und wo ist seine Frau?
21.00 Uhr	Eine Reise durch Südamerika. Die Leute und ihre Sprachen.
22.00 Uhr	Sie lernen einander im Urlaub kennen. Aber wie geht es weiter, wenn der Urlaub vorbei ist?

At what time will you be able to watch . . .

	Time
. . . a documentary?	
. . . a sports programme?	
. . . a love story?	
. . . a detective series?	

4

[Turn over

5. There is a questionnaire about the contents of the magazine. Someone has filled in their answers.

Deine Meinung ist gefragt!

1. Welche Geschichten liest du am liebsten?
   - [ ] Lustige Geschichten
   - [ ] Abenteuergeschichten
   - [x] Tiergeschichten
   - [ ] Liebesgeschichten

2. Die Artikel sind
   - [ ] zu einfach
   - [ ] gerade richtig
   - [x] zu schwer

3. Die Seite mit den Kochtipps
   - [x] finde ich toll
   - [ ] interessiert mich nicht

4. Darüber möchte ich mehr wissen
   - [ ] Umwelt / Natur
   - [ ] Tiere
   - [ ] Technik
   - [ ] Sport
   - [ ] Musik
   - [ ] Kunst
   - [x] Jugendliche in anderen Ländern

What does this person think about the articles?

His/her favourite stories are _____.

He/she thinks the articles are _____.

His/her opinion of the cooking tips is _____.

He/she would like to know more about _____.

6. A girl writes about her own holiday in this area.

> Der Urlaub war toll. Das Wetter war schön und wir haben viele Spaziergänge auf dem Land gemacht. Ich bin auch öfters mit meinem Freund ins Freibad gegangen. Wir wollten einmal Pony reiten, aber es war leider zu teuer. An einem Tag haben wir ein schönes Museum besucht . . .

Tick (✓) **three** of the boxes to show what she did.

3

[Turn over

7. These young people say what book they have read recently and why.

„Der Graf von Monte Christo." Ich habe den Film schon gesehen und mir darum das Buch gekauft.

Daniel

Ich habe gerade „Nero Corleone" von Elke Heidenreich gelesen. Es beschreibt Katzen so schön. Ich mag Katzen sehr.

Sarah

„Die Unendliche Geschichte." Eine Schulfreundin hat es mir gegeben.

Lara

	Book	Why did he/she read it?
Daniel	Der Graf von Monte Christo	about cat and she love cat
Sarah	Nero Corleone	
Lara	Die Unendliche Geschichte	

Marks: 3

8. There is a notice in your hotel room about what to do if there is a fire.

> **Wenn es brennt:**
> - Öffne kein Fenster, wenn es brennt.
> - Versteck dich nie in einem Zimmer oder unter dem Bett.
> - Schließe beim Verlassen des Zimmers die Türen, damit sich der Rauch nicht weiter ausbreiten kann.
> - Wähle die Nummer 112 und sage deutlich, wo es brennt und was brennt.

Write **one** thing you **should not do** and **one** thing you **should do** when there is a fire.

You should **not** _____.

You should _____.

[Turn over for Question 9 on *Page ten*]

9. This article is about how arguments can start.

> **Manchmal gibt es Krach und Streit,**
> - weil man dich nicht richtig versteht
> - weil man dir nicht zuhört.

(a) How can arguments happen? Write **two** things.

_____

_____

The article suggests two ways to deal with your anger.

> - Schreib auf ein Stück Papier, was dich ärgert.
>   Wirf das Stück Papier in den Papierkorb.
> - Geh zu deinem besten Freund.
>   Sag ihm, was mit dir los ist.

(b) How can you deal with your anger? Choose **one** of the suggestions and say what you can do.

_____

_____

Total (32)

[END OF QUESTION PAPER]

1300/407

NATIONAL QUALIFICATIONS 2001

WEDNESDAY, 6 JUNE 11.55 AM – 12.20 PM (APPROX)

GERMAN STANDARD GRADE
General Level
Listening Transcript

This paper must not be seen by any candidate.

The material overleaf is provided for use in an emergency only (eg the tape or equipment proving faulty) or where permission has been given in advance by SQA for the material to be read to candidates with special needs. The material must be read exactly as printed.

Official SQA Past Papers: General German 2001

Transcript—General Level

> **Instructions to reader(s):**
>
> For each item, read the English **once,** then read the German **three times**, with an interval of 5 seconds between the readings. On completion of the third reading, pause for the length of time indicated in brackets after each item, to allow the candidates to write their answers.
>
> Where special arrangements have been agreed in advance to allow the reading of the material, those sections marked **(f)** should be read by a female speaker and those marked **(m)** by a male: those sections marked **(t)** should be read by the teacher.

(t) Your father is working in Berlin for a year. You are going to a German school.

(f) or (m)   **Dein Vater arbeitet für ein Jahr in Berlin. Du gehst auf eine deutsche Schule.**

(t) Question number one.

　　A neighbour tells you about your school.

　　How long does it take to get to school?

(f)   **Morgen gehst du also zum Friedrich-Schiller-Gymnasium. Du brauchst eine halbe Stunde bis dahin.**

(30 seconds)

(t) Question number two.

　　She tells you how to get there.

　　Tick **three** of the boxes to show how you get to school.

(f)   **Du fährst mit der Straßenbahn bis zum U-Bahnhof und dann mit der U-Bahn bis zur Heinrich-Heine-Straße. Die Schule ist dann zu Fuß nur fünf Minuten entfernt.**

(30 seconds)

(t) Question number three.

　　You report to the school office. The secretary asks you some questions.

　　Which questions does she ask you? Tick **three** boxes.

(f)   **Guten Tag! Ich brauche einige Informationen über dich. Wie schreibt man deinen Namen? Wo wohnst du hier in Berlin? Wie lange bleibst du hier?**

(30 seconds)

(t) Question number four.

　　You go to your first class. A boy called Martin tells you about the lessons you have today.

　　Are his comments about History and Biology positive or negative? Tick the correct boxes.

(m)   **Jetzt in der ersten Stunde haben wir Geschichte bei Frau Müller. Mit ihr kommen wir alle prima aus. Dann haben wir Biologie bei Herrn Meyer. Sein Unterricht ist immer interessant und sehr lustig.**

(30 seconds)

Official SQA Past Papers: General German 2001

(t) Question number five.

Martin tells you about the school cafeteria.

Tick Martin's choice for lunch today.

(m) **Heute gibt es zwei Menüs in der Kantine. Entweder Schnitzel mit Pommes Frites und ein Glas Milch oder Salatteller mit einem Becher Joghurt. Ich esse heute lieber kalt.**

(30 seconds)

(t) Question number six.

Martin tells you about two activities the school offers that afternoon.

Which **two** activities does the school offer?

(m) **Bei Frau Klose lernt man Brotbacken, und die zweite Gruppe geht für alte Leute einkaufen.**

(30 seconds)

(t) Question number seven.

Martin tells you why he has to go straight home this afternoon.

Why can Martin not stay at school? Write **two** things.

(m) **Ich muss jetzt nach Hause und auf meinen kleinen Bruder aufpassen. Meine Mutter besucht meine Oma im Krankenhaus.**

(30 seconds)

(t) Question number eight.

After school your neighbour invites you for a cup of coffee. She tells you about her plans for a trip to Scotland.

How are they going to travel?

Tick **two** boxes to show which parts of Scotland they will visit.

(f) **Im Sommer wollen wir einen Wohnwagen mieten und durch Schottland fahren. Die Westküste soll besonders schön sein. Mein Mann möchte auch einige Freunde im Süden besuchen.**

(30 seconds)

(t) Question number nine.

She tells you where they went on holiday last year.

Why did she not like her holiday in Greece? Write **two** things.

(f) **Letztes Jahr haben wir zwei Wochen auf einer griechischen Insel verbracht. Die Reise war furchtbar teuer und es war viel zu heiß.**

(30 seconds)

[Turn over for Questions 10 to 12 on *Page four*

(t) Question number ten.

She tells you what is on TV that night.

Write the correct programme beside each time.

(f) **Um 18.00 Uhr kommt die Tagesschau. Das ist eine Nachrichtensendung. Dann folgt um 18.30 Uhr eine Sendung über Löwen in Afrika. Um 20.00 Uhr kommt ein Handballspiel: Berlin gegen Karlsruhe.**

(30 seconds)

(t) Question number eleven.

She tells you what her daughter does on Saturdays.

What does she suggest you could do on Saturday? Write **two** things.

(f) **Meine Tochter hat jeden Samstagmorgen eine Musikstunde. Sie lernt Gitarre. Hast du Lust, mitzugehen? Danach können wir uns zum Mittagessen treffen.**

(30 seconds)

(t) Question number twelve.

She tells you how her daughter earns pocket money.

What does her daughter do to earn money? Write **two** things.

(f) **Sie arbeitet zweimal die Woche an der Kasse im Supermarkt. Und sie bekommt auch Geld von mir, weil sie mir viel im Haus hilft.**

(30 seconds)

(t) End of test.

Now look over your answers.

[END OF TRANSCRIPT]

Official SQA Past Papers: General German 2001

FOR OFFICIAL USE

G

1300/406

Total Mark

NATIONAL QUALIFICATIONS 2001

WEDNESDAY, 6 JUNE 11.55 AM – 12.20 PM (APPROX)

GERMAN
STANDARD GRADE
General Level
Listening

Fill in these boxes and read what is printed below.

Full name of centre

Town

Forename(s)

Surname

Date of birth
Day Month Year

Scottish candidate number

Number of seat

When you are told to do so, open your paper.

You will hear a number of short items in German. You will hear each item three times, then you will have time to write your answer.

Write your answers, **in English**, in this book, in the appropriate spaces.

You may take notes as you are listening to the German, but only in this paper.

You may **not** use a German dictionary.

You are not allowed to leave the examination room until the end of the test.

Before leaving the examination room you must give this book to the invigilator. If you do not, you may lose all the marks for this paper.

SCOTTISH QUALIFICATIONS AUTHORITY

MCB 1300/406 6/21520

Your father is working in Berlin for a year. You are going to a German school.

Dein Vater arbeitet für ein Jahr in Berlin. Du gehst auf eine deutsche Schule.

1. A neighbour tells you about your school.

   How long does it take to get to school?

   _____

   * * * * *

2. She tells you how to get there.

   Tick (✓) **three** of the boxes to show how you get to school.

   * * * * *

3. You report to the school office. The secretary asks you some questions.

Which questions does she ask you? Tick (✓) **three** boxes.

	Tick (✓)
How do you spell your name?	
Where does your father work?	
Do you have any brothers and sisters?	
Where do you live?	
How long are you staying?	

* * * * *

4. You go to your first class. A boy called Martin tells you about the lessons you have today.

Are his comments about History and Biology positive or negative?

Tick (✓) the correct boxes.

	Positive (✓)	Negative (✓)
History		
Biology		

* * * * *

[Turn over

5. Martin tells you about the school cafeteria.

Tick (✓) Martin's choice for lunch today.

* * * * *

6. Martin tells you about two activities the school offers that afternoon.

Which **two** activities does the school offer?

Activity 1 _____

Activity 2 _____

* * * * *

7. Martin tells you why he has to go straight home this afternoon.

Why can Martin not stay at school? Write **two** things.

_____

_____

* * * * *

Marks

8. After school your neighbour invites you for a cup of coffee. She tells you about her plans for a trip to Scotland.

(a) How are they going to travel? 1

_____

(b) Tick (✓) **two** boxes to show which parts of Scotland they will visit. 2

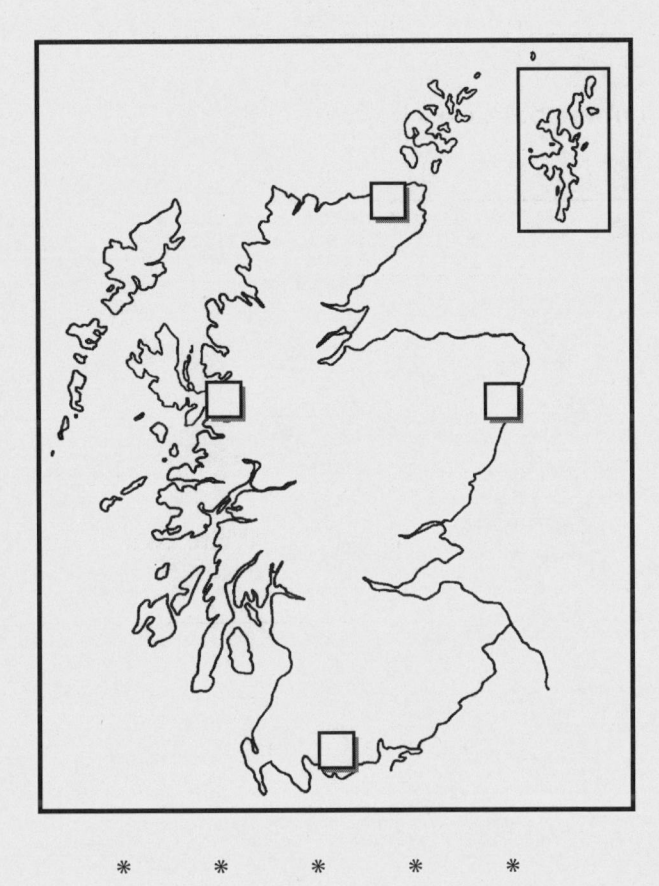

* * * * *

9. She tells you where they went on holiday last year.

Why did she not like her holiday in Greece? Write **two** things. 2

_____

_____

* * * * *

[Turn over for Questions 10 to 12 on *Page six*

10. She tells you what is on TV that night.

| News | Gameshow | Wildlife |
| Thriller | Sport |

Write the correct programme beside each time. 3

18.00 _____

18.30 ____Wildlife_____

20.00 ____Sport_____

* * * * *

11. She tells you what her daughter does on Saturdays.

What does she suggest you could do on Saturday? Write **two** things. 2

_____

_____

* * * * *

12. She tells you how her daughter earns pocket money.

What does her daughter do to earn money? Write **two** things. 2

_____

_____

* * * * *

Total (26)

[*END OF QUESTION PAPER*]

2002 GENERAL

FOR OFFICIAL USE

G

Total

1300/402

NATIONAL
QUALIFICATIONS
2002

TUESDAY, 21 MAY
10.05 AM – 10.50 AM

**GERMAN
STANDARD GRADE**
General Level
Reading

Fill in these boxes and read what is printed below.

Full name of centre

Town

Forename(s)

Surname

Date of birth
Day Month Year   Scottish candidate number   Number of seat

When you are told to do so, open your paper and write your answers **in English** in the spaces provided.

You may use a German dictionary.

Before leaving the examination room you must give this book to the invigilator. If you do not, you may lose all the marks for this paper.

SCOTTISH QUALIFICATIONS AUTHORITY

You are planning a holiday in Germany and are using the internet to get information.

1. This youth hostel might be somewhere you could stay.

BAD DRIBURG

Name	Jugendherberge Bad Driburg
Lage	Am westlichen Stadtrand neben dem Stadion
Anreise	Vom Bahnhof 20 Minuten zu Fuß
Nächste Jugendherberge	Horn-Bad Meinberg — 22km
Bettenzahl	124
Raumangebot	5 Tagesräume, 8 Familienzimmer
Sport und Freizeit	Es gibt die Möglichkeit, in unserem Haus Tischtennis zu spielen. Jeden Tag ist ein kleines Freibad für Hausgäste geöffnet.

(a) Where in the town is the youth hostel? Write **two** things. **2**

(b) How do you get to the hostel from the train station? **1**

(c) What **two** activities can you take part in at the hostel? **2**

2. A mother who has stayed in the hostel with her family recommends it.

> Ich war mit meiner Tochter (5 Jahre) in den Sommerferien in Bad Driburg. Die Zimmer sind einfach, aber sauber und mit Waschbecken. Die Atmosphäre der Herberge ist toll. Es sind immer mehrere Kinder dort, und der Herbergsvater ist sehr nett. Für uns waren die 14 Urlaubstage ein richtiger Hit!

What makes this hostel ideal for families? Tick (✓) **three** statements that are true.

	Tick (✓)
The rooms are very big.	
You can wash in the rooms.	
It is very peaceful.	
There are always children there.	
The warden is nice.	
The warden has children of his own.	

[Turn over

3. You find information about boat trips in the area.

Touren

A	B
• Bootsrundfahrt durch die historische Stadtmitte. Dauer: Fünfzig Minuten • Fahrkarten am Schalter (Schlossbrücke)	• City-Tour mit dem Schiff. Dauer: Drei Stunden • Fahrkarten mindestens zwei Tage vorher reservieren

Tick (✓) the correct boxes.

	A	B
Which tour lasts longer?		
Which tour do you have to book in advance?		

4. You find an online magazine. These young people say what they plan to do in the holidays.

> In den Ferien kommt meine Brieffreundin zu Besuch. Sie bleibt eine Woche.
>
> Dann fahren wir vier Wochen lang nach Griechenland.
>
> *Gertraud*

> Dieses Jahr verbringe ich die meiste Zeit zu Hause.
>
> Wenn es heiß ist, gehe ich ab und zu baden.
>
> *Markus*

> Ich weiß ganz genau, was ich mache. Zwei Wochen werde ich bei meinem Opa in den Bergen verbringen.
>
> Dort ist es sehr schön zum Wandern.
>
> *Katharina*

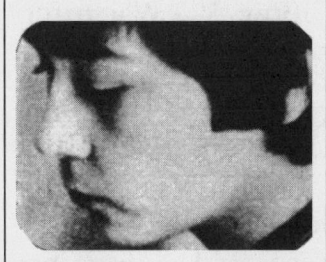

What are they going to be doing? Complete the sentences.

Gertraud's _____ is coming to stay with her.

Then she'll go to _____ .

Markus will spend a lot of time _____ .

He may _____ if it's hot.

Katharina will stay with her grandfather in _____ .

You can _____ there.

[Turn over

5. These girls each say what their greatest wish is, what annoys them, and what they do when they are in a bad mood.

	Mein größter Wunsch	**Was mich nervt**	**Wenn ich schlechte Laune habe**
Katja, 15	Ein Haus im Grünen mit zwei Kindern.	Wenn ich zu viele Hausaufgaben habe.	. . . treffe ich mich mit meinen Freunden.
Heike, 16	Einmal mit dem Auto durch ganz Europa.	Wenn meine ältere Schwester meinen CD-Spieler nimmt.	. . . rede ich mit jemandem.
Martina, 15	Eine Karriere als Sängerin.	Wenn man mich auslacht.	. . . bleibe ich allein auf meinem Zimmer.

Which of the girls . . .

3

	Name
. . . wants to travel?	
. . . does not like it when people make fun of her?	
. . . prefers to be on her own when she is in a bad mood?	

6. In this chat-room on the internet, people are giving their opinions about eating meat.

> **Anna**
> Ich esse überhaupt kein Fleisch. Fleisch schmeckt mir nicht mehr, und ich denke immer an die toten Tiere.
>
> **Joachim**
> Fleisch esse ich, aber nicht gerne. Das ist nicht so gesund. Fleisch ist oft sehr fettig, und zu viel Fett macht dick, finde ich. Das mag ich überhaupt nicht.

(a) Why do they not like eating meat? Write **two** things for each person.

Anna	1 _____
	2 _____
Joachim	1 _____
	2 _____

Pamela loves meat.

> Zu Hause essen wir viel Fleisch. Weil mein Vater Metzger ist, kocht meine Mutter fast jeden Tag Fleisch.

(b) Why does Pamela eat a lot of meat? Write **two** things.

_____

_____

[Turn over

7. Angela and Michael are writing about pocket money.

> Ich bekomme sehr wenig Taschengeld. Deshalb muss ich Zeitungen austragen. Wenn ich etwas Besonderes will, helfe ich im Haushalt.
>
> *Angela, 16 Jahre*

(a) What does Angela do to earn money? Tick (✓) **two** things.

	Tick (✓)
Delivers newspapers	
Works in a newsagent's	
Does her homework	
Helps out at home	

(b) Michael often lends money to his friends.

> Ich verleihe oft Geld an meine besten Freunde. Ich weiß immer, wo mein Geld ist. Meine Freunde geben es immer zurück.
>
> *Michael, 14 Jahre*

Why is he happy to do this? Write **two** things.

_____

_____

8. In this chat-room a parent is talking about the homework club in her son's school.

> Mein Sohn Paul bleibt lieber etwas länger in der Schule. Die Lehrer helfen, wenn die Schüler Probleme haben. In der Schule hat man alles, was man braucht: Bücher, Computer usw. Wenn er nach Hause kommt, hat er dann Zeit für sich selbst.
>
> *Maria Hildersleben*

Why does she think the homework club is a good idea? Write **three** things.

_____

_____

_____

Total (32)

[END OF QUESTION PAPER]

1300/407

NATIONAL QUALIFICATIONS 2002

TUESDAY, 21 MAY 1.45 PM – 2.10 PM (APPROX)

GERMAN STANDARD GRADE
General Level
Listening Transcript

This paper must not be seen by any candidate.

The material overleaf is provided for use in an emergency only (eg the tape or equipment proving faulty) or where permission has been given in advance by SQA for the material to be read to candidates with special needs. The material must be read exactly as printed.

Transcript—General Level

> **Instructions to reader(s):**
>
> For each item, read the English **once,** then read the German **three times**, with an interval of 5 seconds between the readings. On completion of the third reading, pause for the length of time indicated in brackets after each item, to allow the candidates to write their answers.
>
> Where special arrangements have been agreed in advance to allow the reading of the material, those sections marked **(f)** should be read by a female speaker and those marked **(m)** by a male: those sections marked **(t)** should be read by the teacher.

(t) You are going to Germany to spend two weeks in Rosenheim with your pen friend, Martin.

(f) or (m) **Du fährst nach Deutschland, um zwei Wochen bei deinem Brieffreund, Martin, in Rosenheim zu verbringen.**

(t) Question number one.

Shortly before you go to Germany, you phone Martin to check arrangements.

Why can he not meet you at the airport?

(m) **Leider kann ich dich am Freitag nicht abholen. Ich bin bis ein Uhr in der Schule.**

(30 seconds)

(t) Question number two.

When you arrive at the airport in Germany, you ask at the information desk about your bus to Rosenheim.

When does the bus leave? Tick the correct box.

How long will the journey take? Tick the correct box.

(f) **Der nächste Bus nach Rosenheim fährt um elf Uhr vierzig von Haltestelle zwanzig ab. Die Fahrt dauert eine Dreiviertelstunde.**

(30 seconds)

(t) Question number three.

While you are in the waiting room, you hear an announcement about your bus.

What are you told?

(f) **Achtung, meine Damen und Herren! Der nächste Bus nach Rosenheim hat fünfzehn Minuten Verspätung.**

(30 seconds)

(t) Question number four.

Martin calls you on your mobile phone.

What two questions does he ask you? Tick **two** boxes.

(m) **Hallo. Martin am Apparat. Wie war die Reise? Wann kommst du hier an?**

(30 seconds)

Official SQA Past Papers: General German 2002

(t) Question number five.

Martin arranges to meet you when you get off the bus.

Where will you meet?

(m) Ja, wo treffen wir uns? Hmm . . . am besten treffen wir uns vor der Post, glaube ich.

(30 seconds)

(t) Question number six.

On the bus, you chat to a girl who is reading a film magazine.

What does she think of:

horror films?

and romantic films?

(f) Ich habe neulich „Hannibal" gesehen. Das ist ein Horrorfilm, nicht wahr? Solche Filme mag ich sehr. Liebesfilme, so wie „Titanic" gefallen mir nicht.

(30 seconds)

(t) Question number seven.

The girl tells you what there is to do in Rosenheim.

What is there to do? Tick **three** boxes.

(f) Man kann dort angeln, zum Beispiel, oder ein Ruderboot mieten. Es gibt auch einen Park, wo man einen schönen Spaziergang machen kann.

(30 seconds)

(t) Question number eight.

What is there to do in the evenings? Write **two** things.

(f) Es gibt ein modernes Kino in der Stadt. Oder man kann einfach ins Café gehen und Eis essen.

(30 seconds)

(t) Question number nine.

You meet Martin as arranged. He suggests you go to eat.

Where are you going to eat?

(m) Was isst du gern? Ich esse gern italienisch, und ich habe einen Tisch in meinem Lieblingsrestaurant reserviert.

(30 seconds)

[Turn over for Questions 10 to 15 on *Page four*

(t) **Question number ten.**

Martin tells you about a special offer at the restaurant.

What is the offer?

(m) **Im Restaurant gibt es zur Zeit ein Sonderangebot: Zwei Pizzas zum Preis von einer.**

(30 seconds)

(t) **Question number eleven.**

When you arrive at Martin's house, he gives you a gift to welcome you.

What is the gift? Tick the correct box.

(m) **Hier ist ein kleines Geschenk für dich—ein Buch über München. Ich hoffe, es gefällt dir.**

(30 seconds)

(t) **Question number twelve.**

Martin shows you to your room.

Where is your bedroom? Write the word "**Bedroom**" in the correct place on the plan.

Where is the bathroom? Write "**Bathroom**" on the plan.

(m) **Dein Zimmer ist direkt neben meinem Zimmer. Das Badezimmer ist gegenüber von meinem Zimmer.**

(t) **Question number thirteen.**

What does Martin suggest you might like to do? Tick **three** boxes.

(m) **Möchtest du dich vielleicht duschen oder ein bisschen schlafen? Oder möchtest du zuerst zu Hause anrufen?**

(30 seconds)

(t) **Question number fourteen.**

Martin tells you about the plans for tomorrow.

Where will he be going in the morning?

Why?

(m) **Morgen früh habe ich einen Termin beim Arzt. Ich habe Halsschmerzen. Seit mehreren Tagen tut er mir weh.**

(30 seconds)

(t) **Question number fifteen.**

Martin says where you will be going later.

Where are you going later? Tick the correct box.

Why are you going there?

(m) **Später gehen wir zu einem großen Jugendtreffen in der Stadthalle. Meine Band spielt zum ersten Mal da. Ich spiele Schlagzeug.**

(30 seconds)

(t) **End of test.**

Now look over your answers.

[END OF TRANSCRIPT]

Official SQA Past Papers: General German 2002

FOR OFFICIAL USE

G

Total Mark

1300/406

NATIONAL QUALIFICATIONS 2002

TUESDAY, 21 MAY 1.45 PM – 2.10 PM (APPROX)

GERMAN STANDARD GRADE
General Level
Listening

Fill in these boxes and read what is printed below.

Full name of centre

Town

Forename(s)

Surname

Date of birth
Day Month Year

Scottish candidate number

Number of seat

When you are told to do so, open your paper.

You will hear a number of short items in German. You will hear each item three times, then you will have time to write your answer.

Write your answers, **in English**, in this book, in the appropriate spaces.

You may take notes as you are listening to the German, but only in this paper.

You may **not** use a German dictionary.

You are not allowed to leave the examination room until the end of the test.

Before leaving the examination room you must give this book to the invigilator. If you do not, you may lose all the marks for this paper.

SCOTTISH QUALIFICATIONS AUTHORITY

MCB 1300/406 6/21370

You are going to Germany to spend two weeks in Rosenheim with your pen friend, Martin.

Du fährst nach Deutschland, um zwei Wochen bei deinem Brieffreund, Martin, in Rosenheim zu verbringen.

1. Shortly before you go to Germany, you phone Martin to check arrangements.

   Why can he not meet you at the airport?

   _____

   * * * * *

2. When you arrive at the airport in Germany, you ask at the information desk about your bus to Rosenheim.

   (a) When does the bus leave? Tick (✓) the correct box.

	Tick (✓)
11.04	
11.14	
11.40	

   (b) How long will the journey take? Tick (✓) the correct box.

	Tick (✓)
Quarter of an hour	
Half an hour	
Three quarters of an hour	

   * * * * *

3. While you are in the waiting room, you hear an announcement about your bus.

   What are you told?

   _____

   * * * * *

4. Martin calls you on your mobile phone.

What two questions does he ask you? Tick (✓) **two** boxes.

	Tick (✓)
How are you?	
Have you eaten?	
How was the journey?	
When will you get here?	

* * * * *

5. Martin arranges to meet you when you get off the bus.

Where will you meet?

_____

* * * * *

6. On the bus, you chat to a girl who is reading a film magazine.

What does she think of:

(a) horror films?

_____

(b) romantic films?

_____

* * * * *

[Turn over

7. The girl tells you what there is to do in Rosenheim.

What is there to do? Tick (✓) **three** boxes.

3

* * * * *

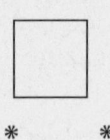

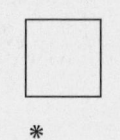

8. What is there to do in the evenings?

Write **two** things.

2

_____

_____

* * * * *

9. You meet Martin as arranged. He suggests you go to eat.

Where are you going to eat?

1

_____

* * * * *

10. Martin tells you about a special offer at the restaurant.

What is the offer?

_____

* * * * *

11. When you arrive at Martin's house, he gives you a gift to welcome you.

What is the gift? Tick (✓) the correct box.

□   □   □

* * * * *

[Turn over

12. Martin shows you to your room.

(a) Where is your bedroom? Write the word "**Bedroom**" in the correct place on the plan. 1

(b) Where is the bathroom? Write "**Bathroom**" on the plan. 1

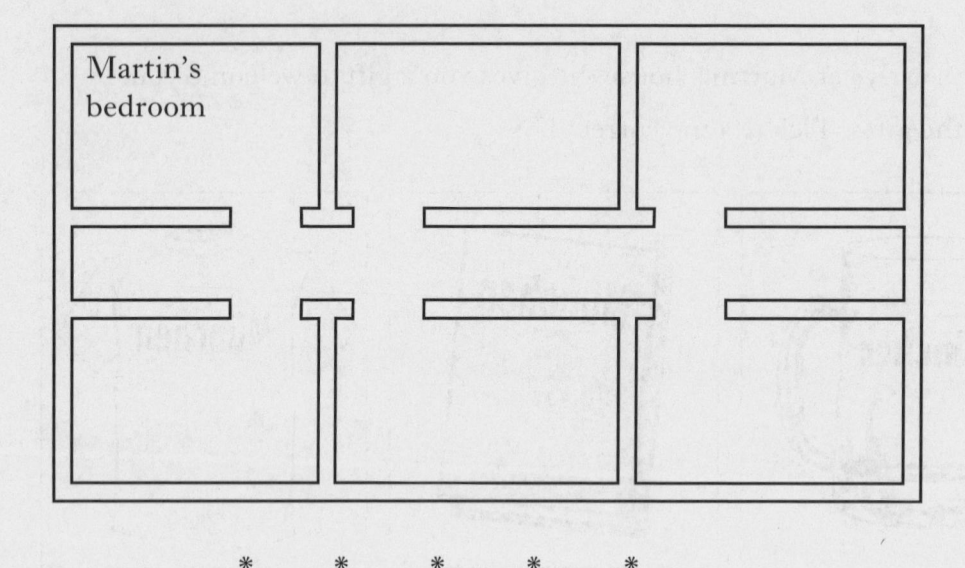

```
┌─────────────┬─────────────┬─────────────┐
│ Martin's    │             │             │
│ bedroom     │             │             │
│             │             │             │
└──┐       ┌──┴──┐       ┌──┴──┐       ┌──┘
┌──┘       └──┐  │       │  ┌──┘       └──┐
│             │             │             │
│             │             │             │
└─────────────┴─────────────┴─────────────┘
```

* * * * *

13. What does Martin suggest you might like to do?

Tick (✓) **three** boxes. 3

	Tick (✓)
Watch television	
Unpack	
Have a shower	
Have some coffee	
Have a sleep	
Phone home	

* * * * *

[1300/406]   Page six

14. Martin tells you about the plans for tomorrow.

(a) Where will he be going in the morning?

(b) Why?

* * * * *

15. Martin says where you will be going later.

(a) Where are you going later? Tick (✓) the correct box.

	Tick (✓)
Youth hostel	
Youth club	
Youth festival	

(b) Why are you going there?

* * * * *

Total (26)

[END OF QUESTION PAPER]

2003 GENERAL

Official SQA Past Papers: General German 2003

FOR OFFICIAL USE

G

Total

1300/402

NATIONAL QUALIFICATIONS 2003

TUESDAY, 20 MAY 10.05 AM – 10.50 AM

GERMAN STANDARD GRADE
General Level
Reading

Fill in these boxes and read what is printed below.

Full name of centre

Town

Forename(s)

Surname

Date of birth
Day Month Year   Scottish candidate number   Number of seat

When you are told to do so, open your paper and write your answers **in English** in the spaces provided.

You may use a German dictionary.

Before leaving the examination room you must give this book to the invigilator. If you do not, you may lose all the marks for this paper.

SCOTTISH QUALIFICATIONS AUTHORITY

SAB 1300/402 6/20170

You are reading a German newspaper.

1. Readers of the newspaper recommend their favourite restaurants in the local area.

Mein Lieblings-Restaurant

Ich empfehle . . .

. . . **„Zum Stern" in Uffing**, weil das Essen dort so gut und preiswert ist.

(Frank Daiser aus Ohlstadt)

. . . **den Alpenblick in Sindelsdorf**, weil Chef und Bedienung so freundlich sind.

(Carmela Eicher aus Weilheim)

. . . **das Jägerhaus in Seehausen**, weil es eine schöne Aussicht hat.

(Hans Schäfer aus Bad Kohlgrub)

Why do the readers like these restaurants? Write **one** reason for each.

„Zum Stern"	
Der Alpenblick	
Das Jägerhaus	

2. This advert is about the attractions at a local water park.

Match the pictures to the descriptions. Write the correct letter beside each description in the grid below.

	Letter
Draußen auf der Liegewiese die Sonne genießen.	
Für die ganz kleinen Badefans: ein Kinder-Becken.	
Herzlich Willkommen bei der Wassergymnastik. Macht fit und Spaß.	
Guter Tipp bei Regenwetter: im Solarium langsam braun werden.	
Hier kann man ruhig sitzen und ein kühles Getränk kaufen.	

[Turn over

3. This article is about summer jobs for young people in the area.

So kannst du in den Ferien Geld verdienen			
	Dog-sitting	**Fahrradkurier**	**Babysitten**
Was ist zu tun?	Den Hund füttern.	Du bringst Briefe und Päckchen von Firma zu Firma.	Spielen, Windeln wechseln.
Was brauche ich?	Du musst unbedingt tierlieb sein.	Du musst die Stadt gut kennen, schnell und sicher fahren können.	Du solltest natürlich Kinder mögen.
Wie bekomme ich den Job?	Mach doch einen Aushang im Supermarkt.	Ruf mal einfach den Manager an.	Du kannst einfach bei den Nachbarn fragen.

Fill in the blanks in the grid below.

	Dog-sitting	**Bicycle Courier**	**Babysitting**
What does the job involve?			Playing with the children and changing nappies.
What qualities do you need to do the job well?		Good knowledge of the town. Ability to ride quickly and safely.	
How do you get the job?	Put a card up in the supermarket.		

4. Three young people write about pocket money.

Ich finde, mit 120 Euro im Monat habe ich genug. Die Sachen für die Schule brauche ich nicht zu bezahlen, die bezahlen meine Eltern. Das Taschengeld spare ich auf meinem Konto.

Ali

Ich finde es nicht schlecht, wenn man sich selbst was verdient. Ich jobbe ab und zu im Blumenladen und verdiene ungefähr 200 Euro im Monat. Damit komme ich dann einigermaßen aus.

Carolin

Ich bekomme regelmäßig Taschengeld von meiner Mutter. Und ich habe jetzt einen Freizeit-Job: Zeitungen austragen. Trotzdem reicht mir das Geld nicht aus.

Eric

Fill in the grid with the correct names.

Who does **not** . . .

	Name
. . . get enough pocket money?	
. . . have a part-time job?	
. . . get money from their parents?	

[Turn over

5. An older reader of the newspaper gives his memories of his schooldays.

These are the questions he was asked.

A	Ab wann durften Sie rauchen?
B	Wieviel Freizeit hatten Sie?
C	Wie haben Sie Ihre Freizeit verbracht?
D	Haben Sie an der Schule Spaß gehabt?
E	Ab welchem Alter haben Sie Ihre erste Freundin gehabt?

These are the answers he gave. Match the questions to the answers. Write the correct letter beside each answer in the grid below.

	Letter
Nur sehr wenig. Ich musste Hausaufgaben machen und zu Hause helfen.	
Ins Kino gehen mit Freunden, schwimmen, Musik hören.	
Ich habe nie geraucht. Meine Eltern haben mir das verboten.	
Die erste hatte ich mit 16 Jahren.	
Selten. Die Lehrer waren streng. Wir hatten viele Hausaufgaben und mussten viel lernen.	

6. These young people write about their main hobby.

Mein Zimmer ist sehr schön und ich experimentiere oft mit Farben und Formen. Meine Kunstlehrerin ist toll: Sie hat immer gute Ideen.

Stefanie

Ich mag Sprachen und bin schon nach England, Japan und den USA gereist. Es hat mich immer interessiert, andere Leute kennen zu lernen.

Arne

(a) Which job do you think would suit Stefanie? Tick (✓) **one** of the boxes.

	Tick (✓)
Nurse	
Vet	
Interior designer	
Policewoman	

(b) Which job do you think would suit Arne? Tick (✓) **one** of the boxes.

	Tick (✓)
Architect	
Tour guide	
Postman	
Firefighter	

7. You read an article about how company bosses relieve stress.

A Ich verbringe die Wochenenden mit meinen Kindern.

B Das wichtigste Anti-Stress-Mittel für mich ist das tägliche Frühstück mit meinem Mann.

C  Ich gehe gern am Wochenende in den Bergen wandern. Die frische Luft tut gut.

D Jeden Morgen laufe ich die 287 Stufen zu meinem Büro zu Fuß.

How do these four people relieve stress? Write **one** thing for each person.

A	
B	
C	
D	

8. You see your pen friend's dad's diary for next week.

23. Montag	10.00 Frau Dr. Stahl
24. Dienstag	Marketingkonferenz, Weimar (Abflug 06.30 Uhr)
25. Mittwoch	12.30 mit der Gruppe aus Leipzig treffen. Gemeinsames Mittagessen im Gasthaus zum Löwen
26. Donnerstag	Frau Peters telefonieren 15.00 Termin beim Zahnarzt. Taxi bestellt (14.45)
27. Freitag	09.00 Besprechung mit Herrn Fischer 13.30 Abflug nach Wien

(a) On what day and at what time is he flying to Vienna?

(b) What is he doing at 12.30 pm on Wednesday?

(c) Where is he going on Thursday and how is he getting there?

[Turn over for Question 9 on *Page ten*

9. Your pen friend's dad is looking for a hotel for his business trip. You see this advert for a hotel.

Hotel Trifthof

- Unser Hotel liegt am südlichen Stadtrand
- Nur 10 Minuten vom Flughafen
- Sie können Ihr Auto auf unserem Parkplatz stehen lassen
- Alle Zimmer mit Bad und Dusche

Your pen friend's dad wants the following facilities at his hotel.

Which of the facilities does this hotel have? Tick (✓) **three** boxes.

	Tick (✓)
Town centre location	
Near the airport	
Parking	
Conference room	
Swimming pool	
Room with a shower	

Total (32)

[END OF QUESTION PAPER]

Official SQA Past Papers: General German 2003

1300/407

NATIONAL QUALIFICATIONS 2003

TUESDAY, 20 MAY 1.45 PM – 2.10 PM (APPROX)

GERMAN
STANDARD GRADE
General Level
Listening Transcript

This paper must not be seen by any candidate.

The material overleaf is provided for use in an emergency only (eg the CD or equipment proving faulty) or where permission has been given in advance by SQA for the material to be read to candidates with special needs. The material must be read exactly as printed.

Transcript—General Level

Instructions to reader(s):

For each item, read the English **once**, then read the German **three times**, with an interval of 5 seconds between the readings. On completion of the third reading, pause for the length of time indicated in brackets after each item, to allow the candidates to write their answers.

Where special arrangements have been agreed in advance to allow the reading of the material, those sections marked **(f)** should be read by a female speaker and those marked **(m)** by a male: those sections marked **(t)** should be read by the teacher.

(t) You are staying for two weeks with your pen friend, Martin, in Germany.

(f) or (m) **Du wohnst zwei Wochen bei deinem Brieffreund, Martin, in Deutschland.**

(t) Question number one.

You go with Martin to the tourist information office to book a city tour.

What two questions does your pen friend ask? Tick **two** boxes.

(m) **Guten Tag! Wir möchten eine Stadtrundfahrt buchen. Wie lange dauert die Rundfahrt? Wo fährt der Bus ab?**

(30 seconds)

(t) Question number two.

Martin tells you there are two places in the town you should visit.

What are these places? Tick **two** boxes.

(m) **Es lohnt sich, das Schloss zu besichtigen. Du musst auch unbedingt das neue Einkaufszentrum in der Stadtmitte besuchen. Dort kannst du natürlich Geschenke für deine Familie kaufen.**

(30 seconds)

(t) Question number three.

You go with Martin to meet his friend, Claudia.

What does he tell you about her? Write **three** things.

(m) **Meine Freundin Claudia wohnt ganz in der Nähe. Sie kann sehr gut Englisch. Sie hat zwei Jahre in Großbritannien gewohnt.**

(30 seconds)

(t) Question number four.

Claudia has just returned from a school trip to England.

What spoiled the trip for her? Write **two** things.

(f) **Wir waren zwei Wochen in Liverpool. Das Wetter war leider schrecklich. Es hat fast jeden Tag geregnet. Und ich habe mich erkältet.**

(30 seconds)

(t) Question number five.

Claudia tells you what they did during their stay in Liverpool.

Put a tick at **three** things they did.

(f) **Wir haben ein Fußballspiel gesehen. Das war toll! Und am Wochenende haben wir eine wunderschöne Wanderung und eine Bootsfahrt auf einem großen See gemacht.**

(30 seconds)

(t) Question number six.

Claudia gives Martin news of her older sister, Birgit, who now lives and works in Edinburgh.

Where in the city does Birgit work?

How do we know she has settled well in the city? Write **two** things.

(f) **Birgit hat eine Stelle in einem Krankenhaus in Edinburg bekommen. Ihr geht es sehr gut: Sie hat schon viele Freunde in Edinburg gefunden. Und sie hat sich eine eigene Wohnung gekauft.**

(30 seconds)

(t) Question number seven.

How often does Birgit come home?

How does she usually travel?

(f) **Sie kommt alle sechs Wochen nach Hause. Sie fliegt manchmal, aber normalerweise kommt sie mit der Fähre aus Amsterdam.**

(30 seconds)

(t) Question number eight.

Claudia's other news is about her cat, which has gone missing.

Which is her cat? Tick the correct box.

How old is the cat?

(f) **Wir suchen seit Wochen unsere Katze. Sie hat vier weiße Pfoten und einen weißen Fleck auf Brust und Mund. Sie ist elf Monate alt.**

(30 seconds)

(t) Question number nine.

Claudia invites you round for a meal.

When exactly is the meal? Complete the sentence.

(f) **Ich möchte euch bei mir zum Essen einladen. Habt ihr am Dienstagabend Zeit? Ja? Gut! Sagen wir, um halb sieben. Ich freue mich darauf.**

(30 seconds)

[Turn over for Questions 10 and 11 on *Page four*

(t) Question number ten.

Martin tells you about a day trip he has planned for Friday.

Where will you be going? Write **one** thing.

What will you do there? Write **two** things.

(m) Am Freitag fahren wir an die Küste—ans Meer. Bring deinen Badeanzug mit. Wir werden bestimmt schwimmen gehen. Wir können auch einen kleinen Spaziergang am Strand machen.

(30 seconds)

(t) Question number eleven.

Martin tells you what has to be done before you can go to bed.

What two things need to be done? Tick **two** boxes.

(m) Bevor wir ins Bett gehen, muss ich noch was erledigen. Ich muss schnell meine Hausaufgaben machen. Kannst du bitte den Tisch für das Frühstück decken?

(30 seconds)

(t) End of test.

Now look over your answers.

[END OF TRANSCRIPT]

Official SQA Past Papers: General German 2003

FOR OFFICIAL USE

G

1300/406

Total Mark

NATIONAL QUALIFICATIONS 2003

TUESDAY, 20 MAY 1.45 PM – 2.10 PM (APPROX)

GERMAN STANDARD GRADE
General Level
Listening

Fill in these boxes and read what is printed below.

Full name of centre

Town

Forename(s)

Surname

Date of birth
Day Month Year

Scottish candidate number

Number of seat

When you are told to do so, open your paper.

You will hear a number of short items in German. You will hear each item three times, then you will have time to write your answer.

Write your answers, **in English**, in this book, in the appropriate spaces.

You may take notes as you are listening to the German, but only in this paper.

You may **not** use a German dictionary.

You are not allowed to leave the examination room until the end of the test.

Before leaving the examination room you must give this book to the invigilator. If you do not, you may lose all the marks for this paper.

SCOTTISH QUALIFICATIONS AUTHORITY

SAB 1300/406 6/20170

You are staying for two weeks with your pen friend, Martin, in Germany.

Du wohnst zwei Wochen bei deinem Brieffreund, Martin, in Deutschland.

1. You go with Martin to the tourist information office to book a city tour.

   What two questions does your pen friend ask? Tick (✓) **two** boxes.

	Tick (✓)
How long does the tour last?	
How much does the tour cost?	
When does the bus leave?	
Where does the bus leave from?	

   * * * * *

2. Martin tells you there are two places in the town you should visit.

   What are these places? Tick (✓) **two** boxes.

	Tick (✓)
Town hall	
Museum	
Castle	
Cathedral	
Shopping centre	

   * * * * *

3. You go with Martin to meet his friend, Claudia.

   What does he tell you about her? Write **three** things.

   _____

   _____

   _____

   * * * * *

4. Claudia has just returned from a school trip to England.

What spoiled the trip for her? Write **two** things.

2

_____

_____

* * * * *

5. Claudia tells you what they did during their stay in Liverpool.

Put a tick (✓) at **three** things they did.

3

* * * * *

[Turn over

6. Claudia gives Martin news of her older sister, Birgit, who now lives and works in Edinburgh.

(a) Where in the city does Birgit work?

1

(b) How do we know she has settled well in the city? Write **two** things.

2

* * * * *

7. (a) How often does Birgit come home?

1

(b) How does she usually travel?

1

* * * * *

8. Claudia's other news is about her cat, which has gone missing.

(a) Which is her cat? Tick (✓) the correct box.

1

(b) How old is the cat?

1

* * * * *

9. Claudia invites you round for a meal.

   When exactly is the meal? Complete the sentence.

   You should come round on _____ at _____.

   * * * * *

10. Martin tells you about a day trip he has planned for Friday.

    (a) Where will you be going? Write **one** thing.

    _____

    (b) What will you do there? Write **two** things.

    _____

    _____

    * * * * *

11. Martin tells you what has to be done before you can go to bed.

    What two things need to be done? Tick (✓) **two** boxes.

	Tick (✓)
Homework	
Wash the dishes	
Set the table for breakfast	
Tidy the living room	
Write a letter	

    * * * * *

    Total (26)

[END OF QUESTION PAPER]

[BLANK PAGE]

1999 CREDIT

1300/103

SCOTTISH
CERTIFICATE OF
EDUCATION
1999

WEDNESDAY, 26 MAY
10.25 AM – 11.25 AM

GERMAN
STANDARD GRADE
Credit Level
Reading

Instructions to the Candidate

When you are told to do so, open your paper and write your answers **in English** in the **separate** answer book provided.

You may use a German dictionary.

Your pen friend has sent you a magazine to read.

1. Two young people write about their plans for the future.

Amos, 18

Ich bin Jude. Nach dem Abitur möchte ich eine Zeitlang in Israel leben, um die Sprache zu lernen.

Das ganze Leben in Israel zu verbringen, kann ich mir aber nicht vorstellen, denn dann müßte ich wie alle jungen Männer dort drei Jahre zur Armee. Davor habe ich große Angst.

(a) What is Amos' plan for the future? Write **one** thing. **(1)**

(b) What problem does he foresee? Write **one** thing. **(1)**

Laura, 15

Ich interessiere mich sehr für Mode. Später möchte ich gerne in einem Modehaus arbeiten. Models wie Naomi Campbell sind heutzutage weltberühmt und verdienen viel Geld. Aber wenn man einen Unfall hat und sich etwas am Gesicht verändert, dann ist alles aus.

(c) What is Laura's plan for the future? Write **one** thing. **(1)**

(d) What possible problem does she foresee? Write **one** thing. **(1)**

2. These two young people write about their hobbies.

Terley, 14

Früher war's doch so: Die Mädchen haben Volleyball gespielt, die Jungs Fußball. Aber Skaten, das tun sogar Leute, die 30 oder 50 Jahre alt sind.

Inline-Skaten überwindet die Grenzen zwischen den Geschlechtern und den Generationen, das finde ich toll. Deshalb wird es noch lange wichtig bleiben, anders als andere Trends, die schnell wieder vorbei sind.

(a) What appeals to Terley about her inline-skating? Write **two** things. (2)

Für viele meiner Freunde ist es wichtig, ein schnelles Auto zu haben. Ich bin aber für Radfahren. In zwei bis drei Jahren kostet der Liter Benzin 5 Mark—aber Luft für die Reifen wird es dann immer noch umsonst geben, genau wie die Muskelkraft meiner Beine. Viele Leute um mich interessieren sich für die Umwelt überhaupt nicht. Mit ihren Autos verpesten sie die Luft. Radfahren ist umweltfreundlich.

Dennis, 17

(b) Dennis prefers cycling to driving a car. What advantages does the bike have over the car? Write **two** things. (2)

[Turn over

Marks

3. The magazine asks: What would you take with you on a desert island?

> Ich muß Post von meinen Freunden kriegen. Also ist ein Briefkasten ganz wichtig. Und weil ich viel Zeit vor dem Computer verbringe, kommt der auch mit. Meistens spiele ich daran, ab und zu arbeite ich auch. Falls ich Langeweile haben sollte, gibt es ja noch E-Mail.
> Zemian

> Mein Kuscheltier, einen kleinen Gorilla, nehme ich auf jeden Fall mit. Wenn ich schon meine Freunde zu Hause lassen muß, habe ich ihn wenigstens dabei. Ich benötige auch mindestens eine Tonne Schokolade. Schokolade soll ja glücklich machen. Ich werde mal ausprobieren, ob das stimmt.
> Adeleke

> Nichts läuft für mich ohne Fernseher. Beim Fernsehen kann ich mich entspannen. Actionfilme lenken mich ab. Zusätzlich brauche ich einen Sportplatz. Meine Gesundheit ist mir sehr wichtig.
> Martin

> Ein paar Bücher stecke ich in den Rucksack. Ich würde viel Zeit haben, und Bücher bringen mich immer auf neue Ideen. Auf gar keinen Fall würde ich einen Fernseher mitnehmen—ich nehme lieber ein Paddelboot mit, um wieder von der Insel wegzukommen.
> Arthur

Each person has chosen two items to take with them:

Zemian—letter box and computer; Adeleke—cuddly toy and chocolate; Martin—TV and sports ground; Arthur—books and canoe.

Why have they chosen these items? Write **one** reason for each choice. (8)

4. A girl called Nicola writes to Claudia, the magazine's agony aunt, about a problem.

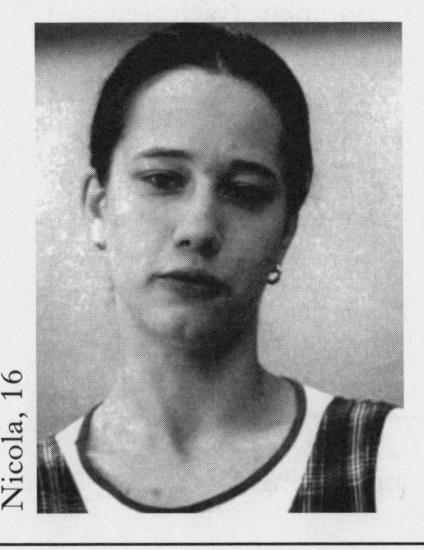

Nicola, 16

Liebe Claudia,
Ich bekomme im Monat nur zehn Mark Taschengeld, aber ich muß jede Woche das Bad und die Küche putzen und in allen Räumen staubsaugen. Wenn ich schlecht saubermache, werden mir fünf Mark abgezogen. Ich helfe aber auch freiwillig im Haushalt, mache Frühstück, hänge die Wäsche auf, usw. Meine Freundinnen bekommen viel mehr Taschengeld und müssen nicht soviel helfen. Das finde ich ungerecht.

(a) Why is Nicola unhappy about getting 10 Marks as pocket money? Write **three** things. **(3)**

Claudia has some general advice about pocket money.

Liebe Nicola,
Ich stimme Dir zu. Ein Teenager sollte Taschengeld bekommen, ohne dafür arbeiten zu müssen. Taschengeld ist wichtig. Dadurch lernt man, verantwortlich mit Geld umzugehen. Natürlich ist es auch in Ordnung, daß Eltern von ihren Kindern Hilfe im Haushalt erwarten. Aber das sollte das Taschengeld nicht beeinflussen.

(b) What does Claudia say about pocket money in general? Write **four** things. **(4)**

[Turn over for Question 4(c) on *Page six*

4. (continued)

Claudia suggests what Nicola should do.

> Vielleicht solltest Du zuerst mit den Eltern Deiner Freundinnen, Nachbarn oder Verwandten reden, mit denen Du Dich gut verstehst und die die Taschengeldfrage nicht so eng sehen wie Deine Eltern.
>
> Hör Dich in Deinem Freundeskreis um, wieviel Taschengeld die anderen bekommen und was sie davon bezahlen müssen. Manche Jugendliche bekommen sehr viel Taschengeld, aber mit dem Geld müssen sie selbst Kleidung, Schulsachen und Ähnliches kaufen.
>
> Überleg Dir Deine Argumente noch mal gut und besprich das Ganze dann mit Deinen Eltern. Wenn Du ruhig und freundlich mit ihnen sprichst, könnt Ihr sicher einen Kompromiß finden.

(c) What does she suggest Nicola should do? Write **three** things. (3)

Total (26)

[END OF QUESTION PAPER]

1300/109

SCOTTISH
CERTIFICATE OF
EDUCATION
1999

WEDNESDAY, 26 MAY
1.30 PM – 2.00 PM
(APPROX)

GERMAN
STANDARD GRADE
Credit Level
Listening Transcript

This paper must not be seen by any candidate.

The material overleaf is provided for use in an emergency only (eg the tape or equipment proving faulty) or where permission has been given in advance by SQA for the material to be read to candidates with special needs. The material must be read exactly as printed.

Transcript—Credit Level

> **Instructions to reader(s):**
>
> For each item, read the English **once**, then read the German **twice**, with an interval of 7 seconds between the two readings. On completion of the second reading, pause for the length of time indicated in brackets after each item, to allow the candidates to write their answers.
>
> Where special arrangements have been agreed in advance to allow the reading of the material, those sections marked **(f)** should be read by a female speaker and those marked **(m)** by a male: those sections marked **(t)** should be read by the teacher.

(t) You are staying with your pen friend, Heike, in Munich. You have each bought a one-week season ticket to allow you to travel around Germany by train.

(f) or (m) Du wohnst bei deiner Brieffreundin Heike in München. Ihr habt beide eine Wochenkarte gekauft, mit der ihr in ganz Deutschland mit dem Zug fahren könnt.

(t) Question number one.

Heike suggests where you could travel to first.

Where does she suggest you go? Why does she suggest this?

(f) Ich schlage vor, wir fahren zuerst direkt in den Norden. Ich habe eine Tante dort, wo wir übers Wochenende bleiben könnten.

(40 seconds)

(t) Question number two.

On the train you meet a German couple. They tell you they are travelling to Cologne.

Why are they going there? What must they do when they get to Cologne?

(f) or (m) Wir steigen in Köln aus. Eine Freundin hat uns zu ihrer Geburtstagsfeier eingeladen. Wir müssen ein Geschenk für sie kaufen. In Köln gibt es gute Einkaufsmöglichkeiten.

(40 seconds)

(t) Question number three.

The train arrives in Cologne.

What is Heike going to do? What does she suggest you do?

(f) Hör mal, hast du Hunger? Der Zug hat hier in Köln fünfzehn Minuten Aufenthalt. Wie wär's, wenn ich schnell aussteige und hier am Bahnhof etwas zu essen besorge? Es ist besser, wenn du hier im Zug beim Gepäck bleibst.

(40 seconds)

(t) Question number four.

Later that day you arrive in Lübeck.

How will you and Heike get to her aunt's house? Write **two** things.

What does Heike suggest you do before you go there?

(f) Mein Onkel arbeitet hier in der Stadtmitte. Er kommt mit dem Auto erst um 17.20 Uhr und holt uns vom Bahnhof ab. Wir haben also fast zwei Stunden Zeit, um uns die Altstadt anzusehen.

(40 seconds)

(t) Question number five.

Later in the evening, Heike's uncle suggests what you could do at the weekend.

What does he suggest? Write **two** things.

(m) Wir haben ein Wochenendhäuschen an der Nordsee. Habt ihr Lust, mit uns das Wochenende dort zu verbringen? Das Haus liegt direkt am Strand, und bei diesem schönen Wetter könnt ihr im Meer baden.

(40 seconds)

(t) Question number six.

During the weekend, Heike says she has a problem.

What is her problem?

What does her uncle suggest? Write **two** things.

(f) — Ich habe mir einen ordentlichen Sonnenbrand geholt. Ich brauche unbedingt etwas dagegen.

(m) — Oh, du, das sieht aber schlimm aus. Ich fahre dich schnell zum Arzt. Er wird dir bestimmt eine Salbe verschreiben.

(40 seconds)

(t) Question number seven.

The next day, Heike's uncle suggests going on a trip.

What are you going to do? Write **three** things.

(m) Wollen wir heute einen Ausflug machen? Die dänische Grenze ist nicht weit von hier. Wir können uns also ein bißchen von Dänemark ansehen und auf der Rückfahrt die Ostseeküste entlang fahren. In einem schönen, alten Restaurant können wir zu Abend essen.

(40 seconds)

[Turn over for Questions 8 to 11 on *Page four*

(t) Question number eight.

You discuss what to do the following day. Heike has friends in Berlin. She wants to visit them.
What does she tell you about her friends? Write **two** things.

(f)   Wir können in Berlin bei meinen Freundinnen Ulla und Susanne übernachten. Ulla arbeitet in einem großen Kaufhaus in der Stadt. Susanne ist bei einer amerikanischen Firma in der Exportabteilung.

(40 seconds)

(t) Question number nine.

Heike tells you where her friends live.
What does she say about their flat and about the district where they live?

(f)   Sie haben eine schöne Wohnung in einem alten Gebäude. Es liegt ziemlich weit draußen und es ist ganz ruhig dort, mit vielen Bäumen und einem kleinen See in der Nähe.

(40 seconds)

(t) Question number ten.

On Tuesday you will be going to Nürnberg on the night train.
Why is the night train a good idea? Write **two** things.

(f)   Am Dienstag können wir mit dem Nachtzug nach Nürnberg fahren. Wir können im Zug übernachten und dabei Geld sparen. Dann haben wir den ganzen Tag, uns die Stadt anzusehen.

(40 seconds)

(t) Question number eleven.

Heike makes a suggestion for the rest of the week.
What does she suggest? Write **two** things.

(f)   Am Bahnhof in Nürnberg kann man Fahrräder mieten. Von Nürnberg nach München sind es nur 120 Kilometer. Wenn wir mit dem Rad langsam nach München zurückfahren, sind wir am Wochenende wieder zu Hause.

(40 seconds)

(t) End of test.

You now have 5 minutes to look over your answers.

[END OF TRANSCRIPT]

Official SQA Past Papers: Credit German 1999

C

1300/108

SCOTTISH
CERTIFICATE OF
EDUCATION
1999

WEDNESDAY, 26 MAY
1.30 PM – 2.00 PM
(APPROX)

GERMAN
STANDARD GRADE
Credit Level
Listening

Instructions to the Candidate

When you are told to do so, open your paper.

You will hear a number of short items in German. You will hear each item twice, then you will have time to write your answer.

Write your answers, **in English**, in the **separate** answer book provided.

You may take notes as you are listening to the German, but only in your answer book.

You may **not** use a German dictionary.

You are not allowed to leave the examination room until the end of the test.

SCOTTISH
QUALIFICATIONS
AUTHORITY

MCB 1300/108 6/12820

Marks

You are staying with your pen friend, Heike, in Munich. You have each bought a one-week season ticket to allow you to travel around Germany by train.

Du wohnst bei deiner Brieffreundin Heike in München. Ihr habt beide eine Wochenkarte gekauft, mit der ihr in ganz Deutschland mit dem Zug fahren könnt.

1. Heike suggests where you could travel to first.
   - (a) Where does she suggest you go? **(1)**
   - (b) Why does she suggest this? **(1)**

   * * * * *

2. On the train you meet a German couple. They tell you they are travelling to Cologne.
   - (a) Why are they going there? **(1)**
   - (b) What must they do when they get to Cologne? **(1)**

   * * * * *

3. The train arrives in Cologne.
   - (a) What is Heike going to do? **(1)**
   - (b) What does she suggest you do? **(1)**

   * * * * *

4. Later that day you arrive in Lübeck.
   - (a) How will you and Heike get to her aunt's house? Write **two** things. **(2)**
   - (b) What does Heike suggest you do before you go there? **(1)**

   * * * * *

5. Later in the evening, Heike's uncle suggests what you could do at the weekend. What does he suggest? Write **two** things. **(2)**

   * * * * *

6. During the weekend, Heike says she has a problem.
   - (a) What is her problem? **(1)**
   - (b) What does her uncle suggest? Write **two** things. **(2)**

   * * * * *

Marks

7. The next day, Heike's uncle suggests going on a trip.
What are you going to do? Write **three** things. (3)

* * * * *

8. You discuss what to do the following day. Heike has friends in Berlin. She wants to visit them.
What does she tell you about her friends? Write **two** things. (2)

* * * * *

9. Heike tells you where her friends live.
What does she say:
(*a*) about their flat? (1)
(*b*) about the district where they live? (1)

* * * * *

10. On Tuesday you will be going to Nürnberg on the night train.
Why is the night train a good idea? Write **two** things. (2)

* * * * *

11. Heike makes a suggestion for the rest of the week.
What does she suggest? Write **two** things (2)

* * * * *

Total (25)

[*END OF QUESTION PAPER*]

2000 CREDIT

Official SQA Past Papers: Credit German 2000

1300/403

NATIONAL QUALIFICATIONS 2000

WEDNESDAY, 7 JUNE
10.25 AM – 11.25 AM

GERMAN
STANDARD GRADE
Credit Level
Reading

Instructions to the Candidate

When you are told to do so, open your paper and write your answers **in English** in the **separate** answer book provided.

You may use a German dictionary.

Marks

Your German pen friend has sent you a magazine.

1. In this article four young people write about anxieties they have.

> Meine Eltern sagen mir fast jeden Tag, das Wichtigste ist, daß ich ein gutes Abitur mache. Eine Zeitlang hatte ich überhaupt keine Lust auf Schule und habe wochenlang keine Hausaufgaben gemacht.
>
> Barbara

(a) How do Barbara's parents make her feel anxious about school? **1**

(b) What effect did this have on her? Write **two** things. **2**

> Ich mache mir wegen meines Aussehens den totalen Streß. Ich vergleiche mich dauernd mit den anderen und frage mich, wie sie mich finden. Nach außen tue ich dann total cool, aber innerlich bin ich ganz unsicher. Zu Hause finde ich mich okay, aber sobald ich rausgehe, fängt es an, „O Gott, wie sehe ich aus?"
>
> Axel

(c) In what ways does Axel worry about his appearance? Write **two** things. **2**

> Ich habe immer Angst, wenn ich einen Jungen mit nach Hause bringe, wie meine Eltern reagieren werden. Meine Eltern meinen, der Junge muß aus der gleichen Sozialgruppe kommen wie ich.
>
> Julie

(d) How do her parents' attitudes to boyfriends cause Julie stress? Write **two** things. **2**

1. (continued)

> Für die Zukunft gibt es so viele Möglichkeiten! Aber was ist, wenn ich den falschen Beruf wähle und das erst mit 25 Jahren merke? Es ist beängstigend, plötzlich vieles selber machen zu müssen.
>
> Peter

(e) How do thoughts about the future cause Peter stress? Write **two** things. 2

[Turn over

2. These young people were asked when they last told a lie.

Wann hast du zuletzt GELOGEN?

Vorgestern wollte ich mich mit meinen Freunden treffen. Es gab ein bißchen Krach mit meinen Eltern, weil ich abends so oft weg war. Deshalb haben sie mir verboten, schon wieder auszugehen. Ich habe einfach erzählt, daß ich etwas Wichtiges abholen mußte, und ich bin trotzdem ausgegangen.

Barbara

(a) Why did Barbara tell her parents a lie? Write **two** things. 2

(b) What did she tell them? 1

Ich habe vorletzte Woche einen netten Jungen getroffen. Ich habe gelogen und ihm gesagt, daß ich keinen Freund hätte, weil ich ihn besser kennenlernen wollte. Wir haben uns dann oft abends gesehen und ich mußte ihm dann doch sagen, daß ich einen anderen Freund hätte.

Monika

(c) What lie did Monika tell the boy? 1

(d) Why did she tell this lie? 1

Meine Mutter wollte mir zum Geburtstag eine neue Gitarre kaufen. Ich habe meiner Mutter vorgelogen, daß die Gitarre 100DM mehr kostet, als sie erwartet hat. So hatte ich dann Geld übrig, um mir neue Kleidung zu kaufen. Ich spiele in einer Band und muß natürlich schick aussehen!

Siggi

(e) What lie did Siggi tell his mother? 1

(f) Why did he tell this lie? Write **two** things. 2

3. Two young people talk about things in their lives which give them pleasure and purpose.

(*Bernhard works voluntarily for the Red Cross.*)

Bernhard ist achtzehn und im letzten Schuljahr. Seit zwei Jahren arbeitet er dreimal im Monat als Helfer bei dem Roten Kreuz. Das war immer sein Traum, seitdem er selbst nach einem Unfall mit einem Rettungswagen ins Krankenhaus gebracht wurde.

Bernhard sagt: „Es gibt viele Menschen, die unsere Hilfe brauchen. Es macht mir große Freude, solchen Leuten zu helfen. Ich bringe zum Beispiel eine körperbehinderte Dame einmal im Monat ins Theater. In der Pause bleibe ich bei ihr und wir besprechen den Inhalt.

Ich habe immer das Gefühl, daß ich auch von ihr sehr viel bekomme. Ich sehe jetzt viele Dinge und meine eigenen Probleme ganz anders."

(a) What motivated Bernhard to be a volunteer with the Red Cross? **1**

(b) What examples does he give of his work? Write **two** things. **2**

(c) How does Bernhard feel he himself benefits? **2**

[Turn over for Questions 3(d) and 3(e) on *Page six*

3. (continued)

(*Sabine is learning Japanese at school.*)

Sabine ist siebzehn und geht in die siebte Klasse in einem Gymnasium. Seit zwei Jahren lernt sie in der Schule Japanisch. „Die japanische Kultur hat mich schon immer fasziniert, sie ist völlig anders als die europäische. Es ist schon ein gutes Gefühl, etwas zu können, was nicht jeder kann.

Man bekommt viel mehr Verständnis für andere Menschen, wenn man sich auch mit ihrer Sprache und ihrer Kultur beschäftigt. Von unserer japanischen Lehrerin lernen wir viel über Jugendliche in Japan, daß man dort viel strengere Disziplin in der Schule hat, als wir."

(d) Why has Sabine chosen to learn Japanese? Write **two** things. 2

(e) What does she feel she gets out of it? Write **two** things. 2

Total (26)

[*END OF QUESTION PAPER*]

1300/409

NATIONAL QUALIFICATIONS 2000

WEDNESDAY, 7 JUNE 1.30 PM – 2.00 PM (APPROX)

GERMAN
STANDARD GRADE
Credit Level
Listening Transcript

This paper must not be seen by any candidate.

The material overleaf is provided for use in an emergency only (eg the tape or equipment proving faulty) or where permission has been given in advance by SQA for the material to be read to candidates with special needs. The material must be read exactly as printed.

Transcript—Credit Level

> **Instructions to reader(s):**
>
> For each item, read the English **once**, then read the German **three times**, with an interval of 5 seconds between the readings. On completion of the third reading, pause for the length of time indicated in brackets after each item, to allow the candidates to write their answers.
>
> Where special arrangements have been agreed in advance to allow the reading of the material, those sections marked **(f)** should be read by a female speaker and those marked **(m)** by a male: those sections marked **(t)** should be read by the teacher.

(t) You are travelling to Austria to go skiing. You arrive at the station in Innsbruck. A ski instructor from your hotel is waiting to collect you.

(f) or (m) Du fährst nach Österreich zum Skilaufen. Du kommst in Innsbruck an. Ein Skilehrer vom Hotel ist am Bahnhof, um dich abzuholen.

(t) Question number one.

He asks you about your journey.
What does he ask you? Write **two** things.

(m) Willkommen in Innsbruck! Das war eine lange Reise von Schottland! Wann bist du von zu Hause weggefahren? Hast du in München übernachtet?

(40 seconds)

(t) Question number two.

He explains why you won't be going straight to the hotel.
Why do you have to wait?

(m) Wir müssen leider noch zehn Minuten hier warten. Es kommen noch Gäste mit dem nächsten Zug.

(40 seconds)

(t) Question number three.

You are at the hotel reception.
What does the receptionist ask you to do?
What does she tell you about your room? Write **two** things.

(f) Guten Tag! Möchten Sie bitte dieses Formular ausfüllen? Sie bekommen ein Einzelzimmer, nicht wahr? Das ist ein Nichtraucherzimmer im zweiten Stock.

(40 seconds)

(t) Question number four.

The receptionist tells you about meal arrangements.
What does she tell you about:
    breakfast?
    lunch?
    your evening meal?

(f) **Zum Frühstück gehen Sie bitte ins Gebäude direkt nebenan. Nach dem Frühstück können Sie Lunchpakete von der Küche abholen. Und zum Abendessen heute gibt es ein traditionelles Gericht aus Österreich.**

(40 seconds)

(t) Question number five.

The receptionist gives you instructions about the evening.
What will you be doing this evening?
What must you bring with you? Write **two** things.

(f) **Alle Skigäste sollten sich um acht Uhr unten im Keller treffen.
Wir werden Skistiefel und Skier anprobieren.
Bringen Sie bitte dicke Socken und ein Foto für Ihren Skipaß mit!**

(40 seconds)

(t) Question number six.

That evening you chat to the ski instructor. He tells you about the types of people he meets in his job.
What does he say about the older people he meets?
What does he say about the younger people he meets?

(m) **Ich komme mit den älteren Gästen sehr gut aus. Sie sind meistens sehr höflich und freundlich mir gegenüber. Die jüngeren Gäste lernen aber viel schneller skifahren!**

(40 seconds)

(t) Question number seven.

He tells you about a trip to Salzburg which is on offer on Saturday.
What will you do in Salzburg:
    in the morning?
    and in the afternoon?

(m) **Es gibt am Samstag einen Ausflug nach Salzburg. Man hat die Gelegenheit, morgens die Sehenswürdigkeiten anzusehen. Nachmittags kann man einen Einkaufsbummel durch das alte Stadtzentrum machen. Da hat man eine große Auswahl an Geschäften.**

(40 seconds)

[Turn over for Questions 8 to 11 on *Page four*

(t) Question number eight.

A German lady gives her opinion of the trip to Salzburg.

Why is she not interested in the trip? Write **two** things.

(f) Ach, das interessiert mich nicht. Ich wohne sowieso in einer Großstadt, und ich finde alle Städte gleich langweilig. Ich würde lieber einen Spaziergang auf dem Land machen.

(40 seconds)

(t) Question number nine.

The instructor tells you about an incident last week.

What happened? Write **three** things.

(m) Letzte Woche haben wir einen fünfzehnjährigen Jungen oben auf dem Berg verloren. Wir haben stundenlang gesucht und konnten ihn nicht finden. Er ist dann vier Stunden später unten angekommen.

(40 seconds)

(t) Question number ten.

He tells you what state the person was in.

What state was he in? Write **two** things.

(m) Als er endlich ankam, waren wir alle sehr froh, ihn zu sehen. Er zitterte vor Angst und konnte kaum mehr gehen.

(40 seconds)

(t) Question number eleven.

Your instructor has visited Scotland. He talks about Scotland and Austria.

Why does he like Scotland so much?

Why does he like Austria?

(m) In Schottland ist man nie sehr weit vom Meer entfernt. Das finde ich toll!
Hier in Österreich sind die Berge viel höher und der Schnee bleibt deswegen viel länger liegen. Das ist natürlich gut!

(40 seconds)

(t) End of test.

Now look over your answers.

[END OF TRANSCRIPT]

1300/408

NATIONAL QUALIFICATIONS 2000

WEDNESDAY, 7 JUNE 1.30 PM – 2.00 PM (APPROX)

GERMAN
STANDARD GRADE
Credit Level
Listening

Instructions to the Candidate

When you are told to do so, open your paper.

You will hear a number of short items in German. You will hear each item three times, then you will have time to write your answer.

Write your answers, **in English**, in the **separate** answer book provided.

You may take notes as you are listening to the German, but only in your answer book.

You may **not** use a German dictionary.

You are not allowed to leave the examination room until the end of the test.

Marks

You are travelling to Austria to go skiing. You arrive at the station in Innsbruck. A ski instructor from your hotel is waiting to collect you.

Du fährst nach Österreich zum Skilaufen. Du kommst in Innsbruck an. Ein Skilehrer vom Hotel ist am Bahnhof, um dich abzuholen.

1. He asks you about your journey.
   What does he ask you? Write **two** things. — 2

* * * * *

2. He explains why you won't be going straight to the hotel.
   Why do you have to wait? — 1

* * * * *

3. You are at the hotel reception.
   (a) What does the receptionist ask you to do? — 1
   (b) What does she tell you about your room? Write **two** things. — 2

* * * * *

4. The receptionist tells you about meal arrangements.
   What does she tell you about:
   (a) breakfast?
   (b) lunch?
   (c) your evening meal? — 3

* * * * *

5. The receptionist gives you instructions about the evening.
   (a) What will you be doing this evening? — 1
   (b) What must you bring with you? Write **two** things. — 2

* * * * *

6. That evening you chat to the ski instructor. He tells you about the types of people he meets in his job.
   (a) What does he say about the older people he meets? — 1
   (b) What does he say about the younger people he meets? — 1

* * * * *

[1300/408]

Marks

7. He tells you about a trip to Salzburg which is on offer on Saturday.
   What will you do in Salzburg:
   (a) in the morning? **1**
   (b) in the afternoon? **1**

* * * * *

8. A German lady gives her opinion of the trip to Salzburg.
   Why is she not interested in the trip? Write **two** things. **2**

* * * * *

9. The instructor tells you about an incident last week.
   What happened? Write **three** things. **3**

* * * * *

10. He tells you what state the person was in.
   What state was he in? Write **two** things. **2**

* * * * *

11. Your instructor has visited Scotland. He talks about Scotland and Austria.
   (a) Why does he like Scotland so much? **1**
   (b) Why does he like Austria? **1**

* * * * *

Total (25)

[END OF QUESTION PAPER]

[BLANK PAGE]

2001 CREDIT

1300/403

NATIONAL
QUALIFICATIONS
2001

WEDNESDAY, 6 JUNE
10.25 AM – 11.25 AM

GERMAN
STANDARD GRADE
Credit Level
Reading

Instructions to the Candidate

When you are told to do so, open your paper and write your answers **in English** in the **separate** answer book provided.

You may use a German dictionary.

You are reading a German magazine.

1. An eleven year-old girl gives an interview about her leading role in a new German film.

Wie kam es denn dazu, dass du diese Rolle spielst?

Meine Mutter hat gehört, dass man für den Film Schauspieler suchte. Sie hat meinen Lebenslauf und Fotos dahin geschickt. Sie wusste, dass ich sowas gerne machen würde: Wenn meine Freundinnen bei mir sind, ziehen wir oft alte Kleider an und spielen Theater.

(a) How did she get the part? Write **two** things. 2

(b) Why did her mother think she would like the part? Write **two** things. 2

Du warst die ganzen Sommerferien im Filmstudio in München. War das anstrengend?

Gar nicht. Mein Vater und meine Mutter haben mit mir im Hotel gewohnt. Und beim Filmen hat man mir immer genau erklärt, was ich machen soll. Das ganze Erlebnis hat mir sehr gut gefallen. Ich hätte noch tausend Wochen weitermachen können.

(c) What made filming less stressful for her? Write **two** things. 2

(d) What does she say to show that she really enjoyed the filming? 1

Ich fand es schwierig, in einigen Szenen, ernst zu sein. Man hat mir gesagt: „Stell dir vor, dein Hund ist tot." Und ich habe mir immer wieder gedacht: ernst bleiben, ernst bleiben, ernst bleiben!

She found it difficult to act in scenes where she had to be serious.

(e) How did she manage to remain serious? Write **two** things. 2

Marks

2. Three young people from a youth club in Hamburg talk about themselves and their views on life.

> Ich bin in Afrika geboren, lebe aber seit dreizehn Jahren in Deutschland. Ich finde mein Heimatland sehr interessant und male gern Szenen aus Afrika.
>
> Wichtig ist für mich, dass man mit anderen Menschen tolerant umgeht. Ich mache mir wenige Gedanken über die Zukunft. Am liebsten möchte ich viel in der Welt herumreisen.
>
> Ricky

> Ich interessiere mich sehr für Mode und ich mache meine eigenen Kleider. Ich ziehe an, was mir gefällt.
>
> Ich finde, junge Leute in meinem Alter sollten schon viele Freiheiten haben, damit sie lernen können, selbständig zu sein. Später möchte ich gern mit armen Leuten in der Dritten Welt arbeiten.
>
> Kristin

> Ich treffe mich gern mit meinen Freuden im Café—wir diskutieren viel über Gott und die Welt.
>
> Gut finde ich, dass man sich für die Umwelt einsetzt—zu Hause bringen wir immer unser Altglas und Papier zur Sammelstelle. Später möchte ich bei den Grünen Politikerin werden.
>
> Heike

(a) How do these young people spend their spare time? Write **one** thing for each person. **3**

(b) What else is important for them in life? Write **one** thing for each person. **3**

(c) What ambitions do they have? Write **one** thing for each person. **3**

[Turn over for Question 3 on *Page four*

Marks

3. There is an article about Alhassane, one of Germany's most promising wheelchair athletes.

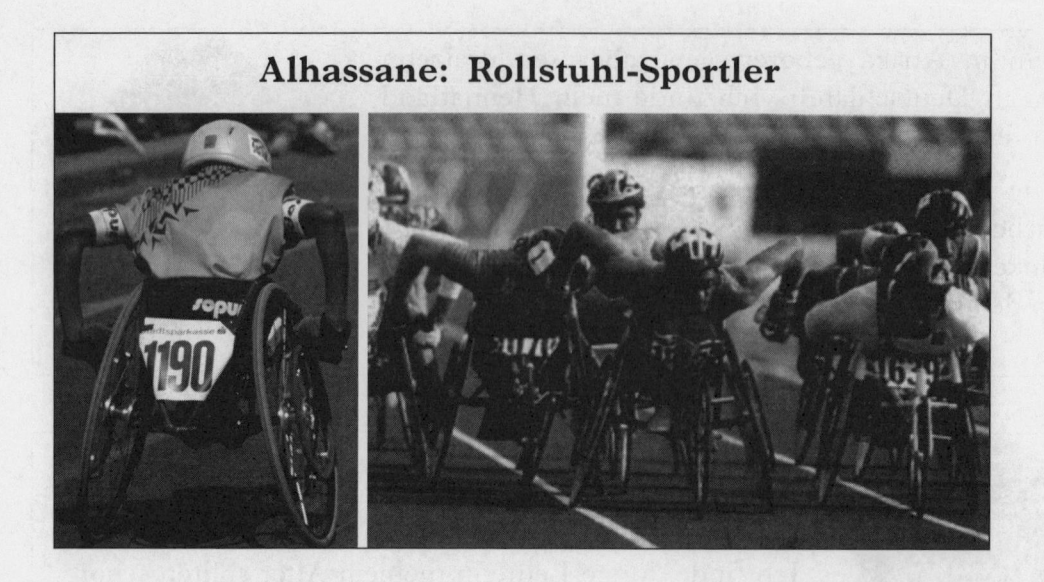

Alhassane: Rollstuhl-Sportler

Alhassane ist so schnell in seinem Rollstuhl, dass er schon in Australien und Amerika an Rollstuhlrennen teilgenommen hat. Und sogar mit guten Zeiten. Bald nimmt er an den Paralympics teil.

(a) What shows that Alhassane is good at racing in his wheelchair? Write **three** things.   3

Für seine Klassenkameraden ist ein Mitschüler im Rollstuhl nichts Besonderes. Bei der letzten Klassenfahrt nach Königswinter am Rhein haben sie ihn den ganzen Berg hinauf geschoben. Dafür durften sie den Rollstuhl ausprobieren.

Alhassane spielt sogar Fußball. Wie macht er das? Ganz einfach. Er zieht sich die Fußballschuhe an die Hände. Denn in den Beinen hat er keine Kraft. Also spielt er mit den Händen. Oder er steht im Tor und hält die Bälle.

Alhassane macht zwar am liebsten Sport. Er geht aber auch gerne in die Schule, wenn es da nicht zu viele Hausaufgaben gibt.

(b) What incident on the last class trip shows that Alhassane gets on well with his classmates? Write **two** things.   2

(c) How does Alhassane play football? Write **two** things.   2

(d) Which particular aspect of school doesn't appeal to him?   1

Total (26)

[END OF QUESTION PAPER]

Official SQA Past Papers: Credit German 2001

C

1300/409

NATIONAL QUALIFICATIONS 2001

WEDNESDAY, 6 JUNE
1.30 PM – 2.00 PM
(APPROX)

**GERMAN
STANDARD GRADE**
Credit Level
Listening Transcript

This paper must not be seen by any candidate.

The material overleaf is provided for use in an emergency only (eg the tape or equipment proving faulty) or where permission has been given in advance by SQA for the material to be read to candidates with special needs. The material must be read exactly as printed.

Transcript—Credit Level

> **Instructions to reader(s):**
>
> For each item, read the English **once**, then read the German **three times**, with an interval of 5 seconds between the readings. On completion of the third reading, pause for the length of time indicated in brackets after each item, to allow the candidates to write their answers.
>
> Where special arrangements have been agreed in advance to allow the reading of the material, those sections marked **(f)** should be read by a female speaker and those marked **(m)** by a male: those sections marked **(t)** should be read by the teacher.

(t) You are travelling to Berlin. You will be doing a two-week work placement there.

(f) or (m)   Du fährst nach Berlin. Du arbeitest dort für zwei Wochen.

(t) Question number one.

You arrive at Berlin-Tegel airport. You ask how to get to the underground station.

What information are you given? Write **two** things.

(f)   Es gibt eigentlich keine U-Bahnstation direkt am Flughafen. Sie können aber mit dem Linienbus zur nächsten U-Bahnstation fahren. Das ist nur fünf Minuten von hier entfernt.

(40 seconds)

(t) Question number two.

You book into the Youth Hostel near the city centre. The warden gives you a copy of the house rules and points out two changes.

What **two** changes does she mention to you?

(f)   Frühstück gibt es nicht mehr um 07.00 Uhr sondern um 07.30 Uhr. Und die Waschmaschinen . . . das Wäschewaschen kostet jetzt drei Mark.

(40 seconds)

(t) Question number three.

You meet two students, Matthias and Steffi, at the hostel. They tell you why they are in Berlin.

Why are they in Berlin? Write **two** things for Matthias and **two** for Steffi.

(m)   —Hallo, ich heiße Matthias.
Ich studiere hier Medizin, weil die Uni hier so gut ist.

(f)   —. . . Und ich bin die Steffi. Letzten Sommer habe ich Matthias in Österreich kennengelernt. Ich habe jetzt Ferien und wollte ihn kurz besuchen.

(40 seconds)

(t) Question number four.

Matthias makes a suggestion for the evening.
What does Matthias suggest? Write **two** things.

(m) Hör mal! Hast du für heute Abend schon was vor? Wir wollten in einer schönen Studentenkneipe was essen. Nachher besuchen wir die Galerie für Moderne Kunst. Hast du Lust, mitzukommen?

(40 seconds)

(t) Question number five.

Your work placement is at the Zoo. You phone to ask how to get there.
How do you get there?

(m) Der Zoo ist ganz leicht zu finden. Wir sind direkt in der Stadtmitte. Du fährst einfach mit der U-Bahn zum Bahnhof Zoo.

(40 seconds)

(t) Question number six.

The manager gives you some more information.
What does he tell you about starting work?
What will he provide for you?

(m) Melde dich bei mir im Büro. Zieh einfach eine Jeanshose und ein T-Shirt an. Gummistiefel und Arbeitskleidung bekommst du von mir.

(40 seconds)

(t) Question number seven.

The next morning you arrive at the Zoo. The manager discusses your placement with you.
What work is there for you? Write **two** things.

(m) Ein Mitarbeiter vom Affenhaus ist heute krank. Hast du Lust, dort anzufangen? Es gibt dort viel zu tun: Käfige saubermachen, Tiere füttern, usw.

(40 seconds)

(t) Question number eight.

Which visitors to the Zoo does he want you to meet tomorrow?
Why might this be a good idea?

(m) Wir haben morgen eine Schulgruppe aus Manchester zu Besuch. Du könntest diese Gruppe begleiten. Dann kannst du vielleicht später Führungen für englische Kinder machen.

(40 seconds)

[Turn over for Questions 9 to 11 on *Page four*

(t) Question number nine.

The manager tells you where you can have lunch.

What information does he give you? Write **three** things.

(m) Die Mittagspause ist zwischen 12.30 Uhr und 13.30 Uhr. Es gibt eine Kantine gegenüber dem Elefantenhaus. Das Fischgericht ist normalerweise sehr gut.

(40 seconds)

(t) Question number ten.

You have arranged to meet Matthias outside the Zoo at the end of the day. He tells you what he thinks of Berlin.

Why does Matthias like Berlin? Write **three** things.

(m) Ich wohne unheimlich gern hier in Berlin. Man kann hier Leute aus aller Welt treffen. Es gibt auch so viel Kulturelles—Museen, Theater und Musik. Und obwohl die Stadt so groß ist, gibt es sehr viel Grün, schöne Parks und Wälder zum Spazierengehen.

(40 seconds)

(t) Question number eleven.

Matthias has a piece of good news.

What good news does he have? Write **two** things.

(m) Heute habe ich endlich eine Wohnung gefunden. Sie ist nur zehn Minuten von der Uni entfernt. Ich habe ein großes, helles Zimmer. Ich teile die Wohnung mit zwei netten Jungs aus Norddeutschland.

(40 seconds)

(t) End of test.

Now look over your answers.

[*END OF TRANSCRIPT*]

1300/408

NATIONAL
QUALIFICATIONS
2001

WEDNESDAY, 6 JUNE
1.30 PM – 2.00 PM
(APPROX)

GERMAN
STANDARD GRADE
Credit Level
Listening

Instructions to the Candidate

When you are told to do so, open your paper.

You will hear a number of short items in German. You will hear each item three times, then you will have time to write your answer.

Write your answers, **in English**, in the **separate** answer book provided.

You may take notes as you are listening to the German, but only in your answer book.

You may **not** use a German dictionary.

You are not allowed to leave the examination room until the end of the test.

Official SQA Past Papers: Credit German 2001

Marks

You are travelling to Berlin. You will be doing a two-week work placement there.

Du fährst nach Berlin. Du arbeitest dort für zwei Wochen.

1. You arrive at Berlin-Tegel airport. You ask how to get to the underground station.

   What information are you given? Write **two** things.   2

   *   *   *   *   *

2. You book into the Youth Hostel near the city centre. The warden gives you a copy of the house rules and points out two changes.

   What **two** changes does she mention to you?   2

   *   *   *   *   *

3. You meet two students, Matthias and Steffi, at the hostel. They tell you why they are in Berlin.

   Why are they in Berlin? Write **two** things for Matthias and **two** for Steffi.   4

   *   *   *   *   *

4. Matthias makes a suggestion for the evening.

   What does Matthias suggest? Write **two** things.   2

   *   *   *   *   *

5. Your work placement is at the Zoo. You phone to ask how to get there.

   How do you get there?   1

   *   *   *   *   *

6. The manager gives you some more information.
   (*a*) What does he tell you about starting work?   1
   (*b*) What will he provide for you?   1

   *   *   *   *   *

7. The next morning you arrive at the Zoo. The manager discusses your placement with you.

   What work is there for you? Write **two** things.   2

   *   *   *   *   *

Marks

8. (*a*) Which visitors to the Zoo does he want you to meet tomorrow? 1

(*b*) Why might this be a good idea? 1

* * * * *

9. The manager tells you where you can have lunch.
What information does he give you? Write **three** things. 3

* * * * *

10. You have arranged to meet Matthias outside the Zoo at the end of the day. He tells you what he thinks of Berlin.
Why does Matthias like Berlin? Write **three** things. 3

* * * * *

11. Matthias has a piece of good news.
What good news does he have? Write **two** things. 2

* * * * *

Total (25)

[*END OF QUESTION PAPER*]

[BLANK PAGE]

2002 CREDIT

1300/403

NATIONAL QUALIFICATIONS 2002

TUESDAY, 21 MAY 11.10 AM – 12.10 PM

GERMAN
STANDARD GRADE
Credit Level
Reading

Instructions to the Candidate

When you are told to do so, open your paper and write your answers **in English** in the **separate** answer book provided.

You may use a German dictionary.

You are reading a German magazine.

1. Three young people describe their most embarrassing moments.

    Sabine had a problem at school with her computer.

    > In der Informatikstunde erlaubt uns der Lehrer E-Mails zu verschicken. Ich wollte meinem Freund folgende Nachricht per E-Mail schicken: **„Ich liebe dich mehr als alles andere auf der Welt!"** Ich tippte die Computernummer ein und klickte auf „Senden". Zwei Minuten später kam mein Lehrer mit rotem Gesicht an meinen Platz. Ich hatte leider meine Lovemail an meinen Lehrer geschickt!

    (a) What did Sabine *intend* to do? Write **two** things. — 2

    (b) What actually happened? — 1

    Jan's most embarrassing moment also happened at school.

    > Auf dem Gang kurz vor unserem Klassenzimmer zog ich aus Spaß meinen Pullover über den Kopf. Meine Freunde führten mich den Gang entlang. Sie machten mir die Tür auf und schoben mich ins Zimmer. Ich fiel mit nach vorne gestreckten Armen in das Klassenzimmer und nahm den Pulli von meinem Kopf. Und dann, oh Schreck, sah ich, dass ich im falschen Klassenzimmer war!

    (c) What did Jan do on his way to class? Write **one** thing. — 1

    (d) What did his friends do to cause him embarrassment? Write **two** things. — 2

    Karl was playing drums at a local disco.

    > Mit meiner Band spielte ich in einer kleinen Disko bei uns im Dorf. Ich saß an meinem Schlagzeug und trommelte so richtig los. Plötzlich sah ich im Publikum ein total süßes Mädchen stehen. Ich war so fasziniert von dem Mädchen, dass ich gar nicht merkte, dass das Lied vorbei war und ich alleine weiterspielte. Da fing das ganze Publikum an zu lachen. Das war peinlich!

    (e) What distracted Karl? Write **one** thing. — 1

    (f) Why was he embarrassed? Write **two** things. — 2

2. These two young Germans have spent a year abroad. They describe their experiences.

Johanna spent a year in Australia.

> Es gab die Möglichkeit, in der 11. Klasse ins Ausland zu gehen. Aber als ich das meinen Eltern erzählte, sagten sie mir, es wäre zu teuer. Dann habe ich versucht, eine Gastfamilie zu finden. Das ging nicht. Endlich habe ich durch eine Austausch-Organisation eine Familie gefunden.

(a) What difficulties did Johanna face before finding a placement in Australia? Write **two** things. **2**

> Am Anfang war ich ziemlich enttäuscht. Ich hatte geschrieben, dass ich zwei Dinge hasse: Haustiere und Sport. Und wo kam ich hin? In eine total sportliche, tierliebende Familie!
>
> Nächstes Jahr besuche ich eine Freundin in Brasilien, die ich in Australien kennengelernt habe. Dort will ich bei einem Kinderprojekt mitarbeiten. Jetzt habe ich Lust auf andere Länder und Sprachen.

(b) What disappointed her at first about her host family? Write **two** things. **2**

(c) What plans does she have for next year? Write **two** things. **2**

Christian went to teach in the United States for a year.

> Ich saß im Flugzeug auf dem Weg nach Amerika. Schon im Flugzeug hatte ich Angst. Ich kannte weder das Land noch die Familie, die mich abholen sollte. Und ich konnte kein Englisch.
>
> Am Anfang hatte ich Schwierigkeiten im Job. Einmal in der Woche musste ich Schüler unterrichten, die einfach keine Lust an der Schule hatten. Sie zeigten mir das ganz deutlich.

(d) What concerns did Christian have on his way to America? Write **two** things. **2**

(e) What difficulty did he face in his job as a teacher in America? Write **one** thing. **1**

[Turn over for Question 3 on *Page four*

3. "Clown doctors" are actors and magicians who work in hospitals in Austria. They help children to cope with being in hospital.

Dreimal täglich lachen

45 Clown-Ärzte arbeiten in österreichischen Krankenhäusern. Sie sind keine richtigen Ärzte, sondern Schauspieler und Zauberer. Sie kommen als normale Menschen ins Krankenhaus. Sie ziehen sich um und erkundigen sich bei den Krankenschwestern über die kleinen Patienten. Sie wissen dann ganz genau, warum die Kinder im Krankenhaus sind.

Ein Clown-Arzt beginnt mit der Untersuchung eines Teddybären. Mit einem Riesen-Stethoskop untersucht er den kleinen Teddybären. „Das klingt ja gar nicht gut", sagt der Clown-Arzt. „Das müssen wir sofort behandeln..." Bald bekommt der Teddybär einen riesigen Verband um den Kopf.

Wenn die Clown-Ärzte kommen, dann verschwindet die Traurigkeit. „Lachen ist die beste Medizin", meint eine Krankenschwester. „Wenn Kinder wieder lachen können, dann werden sie wieder gesund. Die Kinder verlieren ein wenig die Angst vor Operationen".

(a) How do the "clown doctors" prepare for their visits to the children's ward? Write **two** things. **2**

(b) Give an example of what the "clown doctors" do to amuse the children. Write **three** things. **3**

(c) What benefits do the children gain from the visit of the "clown doctors"? Write **three** things. **3**

Total (26)

[END OF QUESTION PAPER]

Official SQA Past Papers: Credit German 2002

1300/409

| NATIONAL QUALIFICATIONS 2002 | TUESDAY, 21 MAY 2.30 PM – 3.00 PM (APPROX) | **GERMAN STANDARD GRADE** Credit Level Listening Transcript |

This paper must not be seen by any candidate.

The material overleaf is provided for use in an emergency only (eg the tape or equipment proving faulty) or where permission has been given in advance by SQA for the material to be read to candidates with special needs. The material must be read exactly as printed.

Transcript—Credit Level

> **Instructions to reader(s):**
>
> For each item, read the English **once**, then read the German **three times**, with an interval of 5 seconds between the readings. On completion of the third reading, pause for the length of time indicated in brackets after each item, to allow the candidates to write their answers.
>
> Where special arrangements have been agreed in advance to allow the reading of the material, those sections marked **(f)** should be read by a female speaker and those marked **(m)** by a male: those sections marked **(t)** should be read by the teacher.

(t) You are going to the South of Germany to do a week's work experience in a hotel.

(f) or (m)   Du fährst nach Süddeutschland, um eine Woche lang ein Arbeitspraktikum zu machen.

(t) **Question number one.**

A member of the hotel staff, Klaus, has come to the airport to pick you up.
Why is he a bit late? Write **two** things.

(m)   Es tut mir leid, dass ich so spät komme. Im Moment fahren viele Leute auf Urlaub. Deswegen gibt es viel Verkehr auf der Autobahn.

(40 seconds)

(t) **Question number two.**

On the way from the airport, Klaus tells you about Schloss Elmau, the hotel where you will be working.
What size is the hotel?
What type of guests stay there and why?

(m)   Schloss Elmau ist ein relativ kleines Hotel mit nur dreißig Zimmern. Im Sommer gibt es viele ältere Leute, die vor allem Ruhe haben wollen. Sie genießen hier die ruhige Lage des Hotels.

(40 seconds)

(t) **Question number three.**

Klaus tells you about his job in the hotel.
Who is he responsible for?
What are his duties? Write **two** things.

(m)   Ich bin der Oberkellner des Restaurants und bin für die anderen Kellner und Kellnerinnen verantwortlich. Ich organisiere den Tischplan im Speisesaal. Ich begrüße die Gäste und führe sie zu ihren Plätzen.

(40 seconds)

(t) Question number four.

Klaus tells you the arrangements for staff mealtimes.
What unusual arrangement is there for Thursdays?
Why does Klaus think this is a good idea, especially for you?

(m) **Einmal in der Woche, donnerstags, darf man mit den Gästen im Restaurant zu Abend essen. Das ist für dich vielleicht besonders interessant, weil du dann die Möglichkeit hast, Deutsch mit Deutschen zu reden.**

(40 seconds)

(t) Question number five.

As you approach the hotel, you hear some athletics news on the car radio.
What are we told about a local high jumper, Heino Günther?

(f) **Meine sehr geehrten Damen und Herren, der Hochspringer Heino Günther trainiert zur Zeit für die Olympischen Spiele 2004.**

(40 seconds)

(t) Question number six.

You then hear the weather forecast for the area.
What type of weather can you expect tomorrow? Write **two** things.
Which group of people is being warned and why?

(f) **Und nun die Wetteraussichten. Der Nebel der frühen Morgenstunden bleibt bis in den Nachmittag. Bis zum Abend können höhere Windstärken bis zu siebzig Kilometern pro Stunde und Gewitter auftreten. Das kann für Bergsteiger und Wanderer gefährlich sein.**

(40 seconds)

(t) Question number seven.

When you arrive at the hotel, the receptionist is pleased to discover you come from Scotland.
Why? Write **three** things.

(f) **Mein Großvater war Schotte, ist aber 1953 nach Deutschland gekommen. Schottland ist ein Land, das ich gern kennenlernen möchte. Ich hoffe, nächsten Sommer mal hinzufahren. Vielleicht kannst du mir einige Sehenswürdigkeiten empfehlen.**

(40 seconds)

[Turn over for Questions 8, 9 and 10 on *Page four*

(t) Question number eight.

A Hungarian guest comes to reception with a problem.
What has happened?
Why is the guest particularly worried?

(m) **Entschuldigen Sie, ich kann meinen Reisepass nicht finden, ausgerechnet heute, wenn ich wieder nach Hause fahre.**

(40 seconds)

(t) Question number nine.

The receptionist tells you that you will be working in reception tomorrow.
What will your duties be? Write **three** things.

(f) **Morgen arbeitest du mit mir in der Rezeption. Wir machen Reservierungen, verkaufen Postkarten und geben Informationen über Ausflüge, zum Beispiel Bootstouren.**

(40 seconds)

(t) Question number ten.

You meet another student, a girl from Sweden called Anna.
Why is she working at the hotel? Write **two** things.

(f) **Ich studiere Deutsch an der Universität in Stockholm. Ich bin nach Deutschland gekommen, um mein Deutsch zu verbessern. Ich könnte mir vorstellen, später mal im Tourismusbereich zu arbeiten. Dafür ist eine Fremdsprache sehr wichtig.**

(40 seconds)

(t) End of test.

Now look over your answers.

[END OF TRANSCRIPT]

1300/408

NATIONAL
QUALIFICATIONS
2002

TUESDAY, 21 MAY
2.30 PM – 3.00 PM
(APPROX)

**GERMAN
STANDARD GRADE**
Credit Level
Listening

Instructions to the Candidate

When you are told to do so, open your paper.

You will hear a number of short items in German. You will hear each item three times, then you will have time to write your answer.

Write your answers, **in English**, in the **separate** answer book provided.

You may take notes as you are listening to the German, but only in your answer book.

You may **not** use a German dictionary.

You are not allowed to leave the examination room until the end of the test.

Marks

You are going to the South of Germany to do a week's work experience in a hotel.

Du fährst nach Süddeutschland, um eine Woche lang ein Arbeitspraktikum zu machen.

1. A member of the hotel staff, Klaus, has come to the airport to pick you up. Why is he a bit late? Write **two** things.   2

* * * * *

2. On the way from the airport, Klaus tells you about Schloss Elmau, the hotel where you will be working.
   (*a*) What size is the hotel?   1
   (*b*) What type of guests stay there and why?   2

* * * * *

3. Klaus tells you about his job in the hotel.
   (*a*) Who is he responsible for?   1
   (*b*) What are his duties? Write **two** things.   2

* * * * *

4. Klaus tells you the arrangements for staff mealtimes.
   (*a*) What unusual arrangement is there for Thursdays?   1
   (*b*) Why does Klaus think this is a good idea, especially for you?   1

* * * * *

5. As you approach the hotel, you hear some athletics news on the car radio. What are we told about a local high jumper, Heino Günther?   1

* * * * *

6. You then hear the weather forecast for the area.
   (*a*) What type of weather can you expect tomorrow? Write **two** things.   2
   (*b*) Which group of people is being warned and why?   2

* * * * *

7. When you arrive at the hotel, the receptionist is pleased to discover you come from Scotland. Why? Write **three** things.   3

* * * * *

Marks

8. A Hungarian guest comes to reception with a problem.
    (*a*) What has happened?   **1**
    (*b*) Why is the guest particularly worried?   **1**

          *   *   *   *   *

9. The receptionist tells you that you will be working in reception tomorrow. What will your duties be? Write **three** things.   **3**

          *   *   *   *   *

10. You meet another student, a girl from Sweden called Anna. Why is she working at the hotel? Write **two** things.   **2**

          *   *   *   *   *

Total (25)

[END OF QUESTION PAPER]

[BLANK PAGE]

2003 CREDIT

Official SQA Past Papers: Credit German 2003

FOR OFFICIAL USE

C

Total

1300/403

NATIONAL
QUALIFICATIONS
2003

TUESDAY, 20 MAY
11.10 AM – 12.10 PM

**GERMAN
STANDARD GRADE**
Credit Level
Reading

Fill in these boxes and read what is printed below.

Full name of centre

Town

Forename(s)

Surname

Date of birth
Day Month Year   Scottish candidate number   Number of seat

When you are told to do so, open your paper and write your answers **in English** in the spaces provided.

You may use a German dictionary.

Before leaving the examination room you must give this book to the invigilator. If you do not, you may lose all the marks for this paper.

SCOTTISH
QUALIFICATIONS
AUTHORITY

SAB 1300/403 6/12470

You are reading a German magazine.

1. You read advice on how to prepare for a job interview. These are some things **not** to do.

> Es gibt ein paar Fehler, die immer wieder gemacht werden. Schlecht ist, zum Beispiel, wenn man eine unleserliche Handschrift hat und trotzdem mit der Hand schreibt. Noch schlechter ist es, auf kariertem Papier zu schreiben.

(a) What common mistakes do applicants make with their letters?
Write **two** things.

2

Applicants also make mistakes with the photographs they send.

> Viele Fehler kann man auch bei Fotos machen. Ganz schlecht sind zum Beispiel Ferienfotos. Die schnellen Fotos vom Passbildautomaten sind fast immer von schlechter Qualität. Geh lieber zu einem Fotografen, auch wenn das etwas teurer ist. Beim Fotografieren sind dezente Kleidung und eine gute Frisur (oder wenigstens frisch gewaschene Haare) unbedingt notwendig. Als Mädchen solltest du nicht zu viel Make-up tragen.
>
> Und vor allem vergiss nicht, auf die Rückseite des ausgewählten Fotos deinen Namen und deine Adresse zu schreiben.

(b) What common mistakes are made with photographs? Write **two** things. **2**

1. (continued)

(c) What does the article advise you to do? Write **four** things. 4

(d) What final reminder does the article give about photographs? 1

[Turn over

2. Two girls describe strange goings-on in their bedrooms during the night.

Lisa's friends were at her house for a sleep-over.

> In meinem Zimmer steht ein wunderschöner Schaukelstuhl*, den mir meine Oma gegeben hat. Eines Abends waren meine Eltern nicht zu Hause und meine Freundinnen übernachteten bei mir. Nach einer gemütlichen Video-Session legten wir uns ins Bett und redeten noch eine Zeitlang miteinander. Plötzlich ging das Licht aus. Wir hielten den Atem an und versuchten, uns nicht zu bewegen. Dann begann der Stuhl, langsam auf und ab zu schaukeln. Doch in diesem Augenblick verlor ich meine Angst. Ich erinnerte mich daran, wie früher meine Oma oft die ganze Nacht in diesem Stuhl saß und auf mich aufpasste, wenn meine Eltern ausgegangen waren.
>
> Lisa

(*der Schaukelstuhl = rocking chair)

(a) How did the girls react when the light suddenly went out? Write **two** things.   2

(b) What happened next?   1

(c) What thought reassured Lisa? Write **two** things.   2

2. (continued)

Bettina describes her spooky experience.

Eines Nachts konnte ich nicht einschlafen. Also legte ich eine Kassette in meinen Kassettenrekorder. Als die Kassette zu Ende war, wollte ich den Rekorder ausschalten. Ich hatte ihn aber aus Versehen auf „Aufnahme" geschaltet. Am nächsten Morgen hörte ich die Kassette nochmal an und da hatte ich Angst. Ich hörte Schritte, als ob jemand durch mein Zimmer ginge. Sofort rannte ich zu meiner Mutter. Sie beruhigte mich. Sie war es gewesen—während der Nacht war sie in mein Zimmer gekommen und hatte das Fenster zugemacht.

Bettina

(d) Why did Bettina put a cassette on? **1**

(e) Instead of switching the tape recorder off, she pressed the "Record" button by mistake. What sounds had been recorded? **1**

(f) How was her mum able to reassure her? Write **two** things. **2**

[Turn over

3. This article is about the fast-food industry in Germany.

> Fastfood ist in. Circa zwei Drittel der Deutschen essen regelmäßig an Imbissbuden oder in Fastfood-Ketten. Das sind elf Millionen mehr als noch vor fünf Jahren.
>
> Zu Hause wird immer weniger gekocht. Woran liegt das? Single-Haushalte nehmen zu, mehr und mehr Frauen sind heute berufstätig und wegen unserer hektischen Lebensweise brauchen wir schnelles Essen.

(a) What two statistics show the popularity of fast food in Germany? Write **two** things. **2**

(b) Why are people cooking less at home? Write **three** things. **3**

3. (continued)

> Für die enorme Beliebtheit des Fastfoods gibt es mehrere Gründe. Ob man ein Restaurant in Tokio, Amsterdam oder Casablanca besucht, ist das Essen das gleiche. Man kann sich darauf verlassen. Die Preise sind zwar nicht billig, aber immer noch preiswerter als in einem normalen Restaurant. Und der Besuch im Fastfood-Lokal ist für viele Familien oft die einzige Möglichkeit, überhaupt einmal mit der ganzen Familie essen zu gehen.

(c) What reasons are given for the popularity of fast food? Write **three** things.

3

Total (26)

[END OF QUESTION PAPER]

[BLANK PAGE]

1300/409

NATIONAL QUALIFICATIONS 2003

TUESDAY, 20 MAY 2.30 PM – 3.00 PM (APPROX)

GERMAN
STANDARD GRADE
Credit Level
Listening Transcript

This paper must not be seen by any candidate.

The material overleaf is provided for use in an emergency only (eg the CD or equipment proving faulty) or where permission has been given in advance by SQA for the material to be read to candidates with special needs. The material must be read exactly as printed.

Transcript—Credit Level

> **Instructions to reader(s):**
>
> For each item, read the English **once**, then read the German **three times**, with an interval of 5 seconds between the readings. On completion of the third reading, pause for the length of time indicated in brackets after each item, to allow the candidates to write their answers.
>
> Where special arrangements have been agreed in advance to allow the reading of the material, those sections marked **(f)** should be read by a female speaker and those marked **(m)** by a male: those sections marked **(t)** should be read by the teacher.

(t) You are taking part in a sports camp for young people in the north of Germany.

(f) or (m) **Du nimmst an einem Sportcamp für Jugendliche in Norddeutschland teil.**

(t) Question number one.

You arrive at the camp. One of the leaders suggests what you could do to help after you have unpacked.

What could you do? Write **two** things.

(m) **Du willst bestimmt auspacken, nicht wahr? Danach könntest du vielleicht den jüngeren Kindern helfen, ihre Betten zu machen. Oder du könntest den Salat für das Abendessen vorbereiten.**

(40 seconds)

(t) Question number two.

The leader then gives you information about the following morning.

Why are you going for a walk after breakfast? Write **two** things.

(m) **Nach dem Frühstück machen wir einen kleinen Spaziergang, damit ihr wisst, wo sich alles befindet: Wo die Tennisplätze sind, usw. Du wirst auch die Möglichkeit haben, mit den anderen Jugendlichen zu sprechen.**

(40 seconds)

(t) Question number three.

The leader asks you about your general health.

What does he ask you? Write **two** things.

(m) **So, jetzt einige Fragen zur Gesundheit. Warst du in den letzten vier Wochen krank? Nimmst du zur Zeit irgendwelche Medikamente?**

(40 seconds)

(t) Question number four.

Later you chat to a girl called Katrin in the TV room. She tells you what she has been watching.
Why did she find the TV programme interesting?
Why does she want to watch the next programme?

(f) **Ich habe gerade eine Sendung über Radfahren in Holland gesehen. Das war interessant, denn ich hoffe, bald in Holland eine Radtour zu machen. Jetzt kommt ein Abenteuerfilm mit meinem Lieblingsschauspieler. Den Film muss ich sehen.**

(40 seconds)

(t) Question number five.

The next morning Katrin talks about her interest in sport.
Why is she so interested in sport? Write **three** things.

(f) **Sport in der Schule hat mir schon immer gut gefallen, weil wir viele verschiedene Sportarten machen können. Ich stamme aus einer sehr sportlichen Familie. Meine Tante spielt Volleyball für die deutsche Nationalmannschaft.**

(40 seconds)

(t) Question number six.

Katrin's sister was unable to come to the camp.
Why was her sister unable to come? Write **two** things.

(f) **Meine Schwester ist auch Sportfan und wollte diese Woche mitkommen. Sie hat sich aber den Arm verletzt. Der Arzt hat gesagt, sie darf im Moment nicht mehr trainieren. Das ist schade, nicht wahr?**

(40 seconds)

(t) Question number seven.

Katrin has been to the camp before. She tells you about the athletics coach, Frau Thomas.
What does she say about her? Write **two** things.

(f) **Frau Thomas, die sich auf Leichtathletik konzentriert, interessiert sich sehr für junge Leute. Mit ihr kommen wir alle gut aus. Wenn man Schwierigkeiten oder Probleme hat, kann man ruhig zu ihr gehen.**

(40 seconds)

[Turn over for Questions 8 to 11 on *Page four*

(t) Question number eight.

What does Katrin tell you about the meals at the camp? Write **three** things.

(f) Das Essen hier ist immer sehr gesund—viel Obst und Gemüse. Am Freitagabend kochen wir selbst. Das macht riesig Spaß. Wenn das Wetter schön ist, essen wir draußen im Garten.

(40 seconds)

(t) Question number nine.

Katrin tells you about the summer job she will do after the camp.

Where exactly will she be working?

Why is she looking forward to the job? Write **two** things.

(f) Ich habe einen Ferienjob gefunden. Ich werde im Verkehrsamt in meiner Stadt arbeiten. Natürlich freue ich mich darauf, Touristen aus aller Welt helfen zu können. Und ich werde mein eigenes Geld verdienen!

(40 seconds)

(t) Question number ten.

You ask Katrin what she plans to do next year at school.

Why has she chosen Computing? Write **two** things.

(f) Nächstes Jahr habe ich vor, mit Informatik weiterzumachen. Ich habe Informatik gewählt, denn ich schreibe gern Programme und verbringe viel Zeit an meinem Computer. Heutzutage ist es für viele Berufe sehr wichtig, dass man sich mit Computern gut auskennt.

(40 seconds)

(t) Question number eleven.

The leader tells you about a party which is planned for the last evening.

What are the arrangements for food and drink? Write **two** things.

(m) Am letzten Abend gibt es eine Party. Jeder bringt etwas zu trinken mit, wie zum Beispiel Saft oder Cola. Und unser Koch backt immer einen Kuchen in Form eines Tennisschlägers.

(40 seconds)

(t) End of test.

Now look over your answers.

[END OF TRANSCRIPT]

Official SQA Past Papers: Credit German 2003

FOR OFFICIAL USE

C

Total Mark

1300/408

NATIONAL QUALIFICATIONS 2003

TUESDAY, 20 MAY 2.30 PM – 3.00 PM (APPROX)

GERMAN STANDARD GRADE
Credit Level
Listening

Fill in these boxes and read what is printed below.

Full name of centre

Town

Forename(s)

Surname

Date of birth
Day Month Year

Scottish candidate number

Number of seat

When you are told to do so, open your paper.

You will hear a number of short items in German. You will hear each item three times, then you will have time to write your answer.

Write your answers, **in English**, in this book, in the appropriate spaces.

You may take notes as you are listening to the German, but only in this paper.

You may **not** use a German dictionary.

You are not allowed to leave the examination room until the end of the test.

Before leaving the examination room you must give this book to the invigilator. If you do not, you may lose all the marks for this paper.

SCOTTISH QUALIFICATIONS AUTHORITY

SAB 1300/408 6/12470

You are taking part in a sports camp for young people in the north of Germany.

Du nimmst an einem Sportcamp für Jugendliche in Norddeutschland teil.

1. You arrive at the camp. One of the leaders suggests what you could do to help after you have unpacked.
   What could you do? Write **two** things.

   * * * * *

2. The leader then gives you information about the following morning.
   Why are you going for a walk after breakfast? Write **two** things.

   * * * * *

3. The leader asks you about your general health.
   What does he ask you? Write **two** things.

   * * * * *

4. Later you chat to a girl called Katrin in the TV room. She tells you what she has been watching.
   (a) Why did she find the TV programme interesting?

   (b) Why does she want to watch the next programme?

   * * * * *

5. The next morning Katrin talks about her interest in sport.
Why is she so interested in sport? Write **three** things.

* * * * *

6. Katrin's sister was unable to come to the camp.
Why was her sister unable to come? Write **two** things.

* * * * *

7. Katrin has been to the camp before. She tells you about the athletics coach, Frau Thomas.
What does she say about her? Write **two** things.

* * * * *

8. What does Katrin tell you about the meals at the camp? Write **three** things.

* * * * *

[Turn over for Questions 9, 10 and 11 on *Page four*

9. Katrin tells you about the summer job she will do after the camp.

(a) Where exactly will she be working? **1**

(b) Why is she looking forward to the job? Write **two** things. **2**

* * * * *

10. You ask Katrin what she plans to do next year at school.
Why has she chosen Computing? Write **two** things. **2**

* * * * *

11. The leader tells you about a party which is planned for the last evening.
What are the arrangements for food and drink? Write **two** things. **2**

* * * * *

Total (25)

[END OF QUESTION PAPER]

German Credit Level
Reading 2002

1. (a)
   - Send {love-letter / message / e-mail} to (boy) friend/
     Write to friend
   - Say she loved him more than anyone/anything/
     I love you more than the world/ most in the world/
     more than all the others

   (b)
   - Sent message to teacher (by mistake)/Teacher got message

   (c)
   - Pulled {top / pullover over head}

   (d) Any **two** of:
   - Led him along (corridor)/Took him
   - Pulled/pushed him into (wrong) class/room/Made him fall into room
   - He ended up in wrong room

   (e)
   - Girl (in audience)/A wee cracker/A totally hot lady

   (f)
   - Continued playing after song ended/He was left playing alone/Carried on playing late/Didn't notice that song was finished
   - Everyone laughed/Audience laughed

2. (a)
   - Parents said it was (too) expensive/It was (too) expensive for her parents/parents couldn't afford the trip
   - Could not find {host / guest} family/She had to find a family/Hard to find a host family

   (b)
   - Her application said/She had written that she didn't like sport and pets/animals
   - {They / Family liked} {these things / sport and animals}

   (c)
   - {Stay with / Visit a friend in Brazil/Visit Brazilian friend(s)}
   - Work on a project helping children/ Work with children/Work on a children's project/To do a children's project/ Setting up children's projects/Work for a children's organisation (or group)

   (d)
   - Didn't know {land / country/family/Meeting family}
   - Couldn't speak English/Knows little English/Couldn't do English/Doesn't know enough English

   (e)
   - {Students / Pupils} didn't want to be in school/
     Pupils had no interest in school/
     Pupils were unenthusiastic/Pupils didn't want to learn

3. (a)
   - They change their clothes/Get dressed/dress up (as doctors)
   - Find out (from nurses) about children/why children are in hospital/They ask about the children/They learn about the patients/They know why the children are in hospital/Ask about a particular patient/Ask about (nurses and) children

   (b) Any **three** of:
   - {Examine / Listen to teddy-bear/Pretend teddy-bears are patients}
   - With a huge stethoscope
   - Say it doesn't sound good/must do something
   - Bandage bear's head/Put a {plaster / bandage on/} Bandage bear/Puts on a teddy-bear bandage

   (c)
   - Children's sadness disappears/Children begin to laugh again/Makes them feel happy/Cheers them up/Ward is a happier place/Children don't feel unhappy
   - Children's health/condition improves/They get better
   - They are less afraid of operations/No fear of operations/Keeps mind off operations/Makes them more at ease with operation/They forget about operations

German Credit Level
Listening 2002

1.
   - (Lots of) people are (going) on holiday/
     It's the {holidays/Lots of tourists / a holiday}
   - (Lots of) traffic (on motorway)/Caught in traffic/Traffic jam/Hold up on the road (or motorway)/He was in traffic/Traffic was bad/Motorway was busy/Autobahn was busy/Roads were busy

2. (a)
   - {Quite small/30 rooms / Relatively} Small(est) with 30 rooms

   (b)
   - Old(er) people/Elderly people/Retired/old couples
   - Like peace/Enjoy quiet location/One of the most peaceful hotels in the area/Quiet (in the mountains)/It's a quiet hotel/More quiet than other hotels

3. (a)
   - Waiter(s) (and waitresses)/Serving staff/Restaurant staff/People who work in the restaurant/Head waiter/Instructs waiters and waitresses

German Credit Level
Listening 2002 (cont.)

3. (cont.)

(b) Any **two** of:
- Organises tables/seating/Decides layout of tables/Makes the table plan/Organises table places
- Greets guests/Makes guests welcome/Welcomes guests
- Takes guests to { seats/Seats guests / tables / places

4. (a)
- Eat with guests/Eat in the restaurant/Have tea in restaurant/Eat at same time as guests

(b)
- Can speak German/Learn German/Help you with your German/Hear German/Practise your German/Get to learn language better/talk to Germans

5.
- Is { training for Olympics / practising / preparing

6. (a) Any **two** of:
EITHER
- { High / Strong winds/Very windy OR winds up to 70k/while getting stronger (Ignore wrong time of day)
- Storms/Hurricanes/Thunder/Thunder and lightning
- Mist/Fog

(b)
- Climbers/Walkers/Hillwalkers/Hikers/Ramblers/Mountaineer/People in the hills
- Dangerous/Unsafe/Not safe/Poor visibility/Dangerous conditions/Bad weather/Poor conditions.

7. Any **three** of:
- Grandfather { is / was } { British / Scottish/Grandfather came from Scotland/Grandfather used to live there
- Would like to { get to know Scotland / learn about Scotland
- Hopes to go (next) summer/Will go (next) summer/Hopes to go next year/Goes to Scotland in the summer
- You could advise on what to see/Wants to know what she could see/You could tell her about Scotland

8. (a)
- Lost/can't find passport/ID card/Misplaced passport

(b)
- Is going home/Leaving (today)/Needs it to travel home/Can't get home/Won't get back into this country (ignore wrong day/tomorrow/wrong country)

9.
- { Deal with / Take bookings/reservations/Give people rooms/Check people in
- Sell (post)cards
- Give information about trips/what to do/Give information about boats/Travel information/Tourist information/Get information about trips/Sell tickets for excursions/Give information about departure times/Give information about the area

10. Any **two** of:
- To improve German/She studies German/To learn German/To learn about the language
- Wants to/may work in tourism/Work with tourists/She's interested in tourism/Likes working with tourists/Wants to work in tourists office/as a tourist guide/tourist operator
- Languages are important

German Credit Level
Reading 2003

1. (a)
- Illegible/poor/bad/not good/untidy handwriting/Writing application by hand if your writing is bad/if you have illegible handwriting/Forget to use good handwriting/Make their handwriting untidy
- Using squared/square/checked/chequered paper

(b) Any **two** from:
- Using holiday photos
- Using passport photos/photos from machines
- They are (generally) bad quality
(using bad quality passport photos = 2 points)

(c)
- Go to/get/hire a photographer
- Wear appropriate/decent/respectable/tasteful/discreet/nice/good clothes/Dress appropriately
- Have a good hairstyle/haircut/Go to the hairdresser's/Get your hair done/Wash your hair/Have freshly washed hair/Freshen your hair/Style your hair/Have a good hair-do/See to your hair
- (Girls/women) shouldn't/don't wear too much/a lot of make-up/People wear too much make-up

(d) Put your name and address on the back

2. (a)
- Held breath/Tried not to breathe/Did not breathe/Stopped breathing/Their breathing halted
- Tried not to move/Did not move/Did not want to move/Never moved/Froze/Stood still

(b) Chair/stool began to rock/sway/swing/move (to and fro)

(c)
- Grandmother/Grandmother's spirit or ghost (used to sit) in the chair/stool
- Baby-sat/Watched her/Looked over her/Looked after her/When parents were away/out

(d) Could not sleep/To help her sleep/Trying to sleep

(e) Footsteps/steps/feet (going across the room)/Someone walking/going about/moving (in her room)/Someone in her room/Steps going through/around her room/Someone coming into her room

(f)
- Mother had come into her room (in the night)/It was her
- Had closed/locked window

3. (a)
- (About) Two-thirds (of Germans) eat at snack bars/in fast food restaurants/fast food regularly/Two thirds order fast-food regularly
- 11 million more than 5 years ago/in/over the last 5 years

(b)
- (There are more) single households/people
- (More) women/wives/mums are working/employed/have jobs/don't stay at home any more
- Our life (-style) is hectic/busy

(c)
- Is same (all over the world/everywhere)/(in Tokyo, Amsterdam and Casablanca)/Can depend on it being the same (everywhere)
- (Prices are) cheaper (than in normal restaurants)
- (May be only opportunity for) family to eat together/eat out/Suitable for/good for all the family/families/Lots of families eat there/Whole family can eat fast-food/Whole families eat together

German Credit Level
Listening 2003

1.
- Help (younger children) to make beds/sort beds/Help make beds for younger children
- Prepare (evening) dinner/tea/meal/Make salad (for evening meal)/(for tonight)
- Prepare/something to eat/food (for evening meal)/Help with meal/Help get ready for meal at night/Make their dinner/Get ready for the meal/Help us get ready for dinner

2.
- So you know where everything is/where to find things/So you know where tennis courts are/So you get to know the camp/So you can see the camp/To show where things are/To show you around/To get to know the place/For a show around the ground/To get to know the area/To check out the tennis courts/To look at the facilities/To see the tennis place
- So you can talk to/meet/speak to/get to know other (young) people/others/children

3.
- Have you been ill in the last four weeks/recently/in the last few weeks?/When were you ill in the last four weeks?
- Are you taking any drugs/medicines/tablets/pills (at the moment)?/Are you on medication?/Do you need medication?/Do you have medication?/What medication do you take?

4. (a) Wants to/hopes to/would like to/intends to/is going to do cycling trip in Holland/Wants to go on her bike to Holland

(b) Is (a film with) her favourite actor/filmstar/actress

5. Any **three** from:
- Likes sport in school/Sport in school is/was good/Sport in school got her interested
- Can take part in lots of sports at school/She has many/different sports at school/She does it at school a lot
- Her family is (very) athletic/sporty/into sport/Her family plays a lot of sport/Comes from a sporty family/Sport runs in her family/There is a lot of sport in her family/Family is good at sport/Family likes sport
- Aunt plays/played (volleyball) for national team/Germany/internationally/the German ladies team/the German team/the German national team/for a nation team/for German nationals

6.
- Hurt/injured/sprained her arm/sore arm/Problem(s) with her arm/Fell and hurt her arm
- Doctor/hospital says she mustn't do exercise/sport/train/advised her not to go

7. Any **two** from:
- Is interested/takes a great interest in/has (lots of) time for them/young people
- They/she get(s) on well with her/Gets on well with/is good with young people
- Can go to her with problems/Easy to speak to about difficulties/She helps with problems/Helped her with a problem/Interested in their problems

8.
- Is healthy/(lots of) fruit/vegetables/Is good for you
- The young people cook on Friday (evening)/They cook themselves on Friday/They help to cook/prepare/make meals on Friday/She cooks for herself on Friday (ignore wrong meal time, eg lunch)
- Eat outside/in garden when weather is good/sunny/hot

German Credit Level
Listening 2003 (cont.)

9. (*a*) Tourist office/(tourist) information centre/board/Tourist shop (in her town/where she lives)/Information point/Information kiosk/Tourist place

(*b*) • Will be helping tourists/people from all over world/from foreign countries

• Will be earning/getting/making (her own) money/Will be getting paid/Wants to earn money/Will have her own money/Looking forward to the money/The money

10. Any **two** from:
• Writes/makes programmes/Likes/enjoys writing programmes/Wants to (be able to)/Will get to write programmes/programme computers/So that she can write programmes

• Spends (a lot of) time at computer/She uses her computer a lot

• Important for (many) jobs/It's good to know how to use them for jobs/Useful for (her) career

11. • Each person/you should bring something to drink/cola/juice/Bring your own drink

• Cook will bake a cake (in shape of tennis racquet)/The cake will be in the shape of a tennis racquet/Tennis cake to eat

Official SQA answers to 1-84372-096-5
1999–2003

Pocket answer section for SQA Standard Grade German General and Credit Levels 1999 to 2003

© 2003 Scottish Qualifications Authority, All Rights Reserved
Published by Leckie & Leckie Ltd, 8 Whitehill Terrace, St Andrews, Scotland, KY16 8RN
tel: 01334 475656, fax: 01334 477392, enquiries@leckieandleckie.co.uk, www.leckieandleckie.co.uk

An underlining indicates that a particular word or idea must be present in the answer for the answer to be acceptable eg <u>Friend's</u> <u>birthday</u> (party) — separate underlinings of "Friend's" and "birthday" indicate that the candidate must show understanding not only that this was a <u>birthday</u> party, but that the party was for a <u>friend</u>.

By similar token, a phrase such as "<u>from all over Europe</u>" should be underlined as a phrase (and not as single words, ie "<u>from</u> <u>all</u> <u>over</u> <u>Europe</u>"), as it is the phrase and not the individual words which are important.

German General Level Reading 1999

1. *Main hobby*
   Swimming

   Her dream
   Travel (round) <u>the world</u>/ <u>World</u> tour

   Worst fault
   (Very) Lazy

   Best quality
   Gets on well with friend(s)/Idea that <u>she</u> is a good friend

2.
	Letter
Where could you buy a tracksuit?	A
Which shop is open every day?	C

3. *Day 1*
   - Leave Hamburg/Arrive in Newcastle/Fly to Newcastle
   - Drive/travel to <u>Edinburgh</u>/<u>capital</u>/Stay overnight

   Day 3
   - <u>Hike</u>/<u>walk</u> in <u>Highland(s)</u>/<u>mountains</u>
   - *Evening* <u>Eat</u>/<u>meal</u> in <u>castle</u>/<u>Dinner</u> in <u>big house</u>/<u>palace</u>

   Day 5
   - <u>Shopping</u> (in Inverness)/<u>window-shopping</u>
   - (Go to) <u>garden(s)</u>

4. EITHER: *Mafia*
   - <u>Black hat</u> and (sun) <u>glasses</u>
   - Italian (food) <u>and</u> <u>red</u> wine/pasta and <u>red</u> wine
   - (Use) <u>water pistols</u>/<u>gun</u>

   OR: *Holiday*
   - Shorts <u>and</u> shirt/top
   - Grill/barbecue <u>and</u> lemonade/fizzy drinks
   - Bike trip/Go to beach/bike tour (of beach)

5. (a) *Constanze*
   - Is lonely/on her own (at home)/Likes school

   Franz
   - Has to help <u>at home</u>/Has to do <u>house</u>work/Has to wash up/Has to prepare meal

   (b) *Sebastian*
   - Goes (on holiday) <u>to</u> <u>Spain</u>/with family/Can be with <u>Spanish</u> friend(s)

6. C B A

7. You can use the card in 65 countries.
   You can also use it in Germany.
   You can buy it at the post office.

8.
	Name
People must take me the way I am.	Klaus
Happy people are beautiful people.	Wibke
It's more important to **be** nice than to **look** nice.	Thomas
It makes me feel better if I try to look good.	Andrea
Hair style and colour are important.	Peter

9. (a) Any **two** of:
   - Came out of water (5 times)/Jumped out of water
   - Breathed <u>deeply</u>/<u>heavily</u>/<u>hard</u>
   - Swam <u>in front of</u> boat

   (b)
   - <u>15 metre(s)</u> (long)/around <u>15 metres</u>

   (c)
   - Thursday/(middle of) <u>Next</u> day/In the morning

German General Level Listening 1999

1. - Quarter to eight/7.45

2. - Math(s)

3. - Bike
   - Train
   - On foot

4. - Watch him playing handball
   - Visit harbour

5. - Orangeade/<u>Orange</u> (juice)

German General Level
Listening 1999 (cont.)

6. (a) • Go to music group/Practice in town hall
   (b) • (Christmas) concert/Performance/Christmas

7. • Inge – student
   • Friedel – chemist
   • Petra – school pupil

8. • Engineer on MS Hamburg/Works on a ship

9. • One week in two/Every second week

10. • *Saturday morning* – Go to Hamburg/Go to ship
    • *Saturday lunchtime* – Have lunch on ship
    • *Saturday afternoon* – Take the underground/go to city centre

11. • (Go to) cinema
    • Stay (night) with brother/Friedel

12. • We're all coming to Hamburg tomorrow.
    • We will arrive on Saturday.

13. • (Ice)-skating

14. • Go for a walk
    • See town
    • Have coffee and cake (with Friedel)

German General Level
Reading 2000

1. It is friendly.

2. *Sven*
   Delivering newspapers/Newspaper run/round/Paper delivery boy/Delivering friend's papers/A paper job
   Earned a lot/Got 50DM (for 3 hours)/Paid a lot (for 3 hours)/Good money/Good pay

   Daniel
   Selling ice-cream/ice-cream man/ice-seller/ice-cream shop/
   ice-cream assistant/
   Ice-cream stand/parlour
   Got sun tan/He was in the sun/ He got brown/Sunshine/It was sunny/
   He got sunburnt

   Anne
   Babysitting and doing housework
   Looking after children and helped to clean
   Likes children/Likes the kids/
   Children are nice/She got to work with children/Likes working with children/Likes playing with children/Likes children

3. Plays football
   Sails/Yachts
   Reads
   People who eat with mouth open/
   People who open their mouths when eating

4. Tick at upper left-hand box

5. *First half*
   Sunny
   Hot/Warm/High temperatures
   Summery weather/As in July/
   Same as July

   Second half
   Cooler/Colder/Lower temperatures/Temperature drops/
   Thermometer shrinks
   Rain/Wet/Fair chance of rain/
   Wetter

6. 1st box
   3rd box
   6th box

7. *Markus*
   Adults listen (to his problems)/
   Wish adults would listen/Wishes he could talk to a grown-up when he has problems/Adults are meant to listen

   Steffi
   Children live without fear of war/bombs/
   Children live in fear of the bomb/Children don't worry about bombing/Children shouldn't be afraid of bombs

   Elmar
   Better/(more) interesting job/
   Better workspace

   Inge
   School starts later/have longer holidays/Wish school was shorter/
   Less time in school/School was not so long

8. (a) e-mail address/web address/
       your e-mail address
   (b) web-site/www.adresse.de/internet (site)

9. 3
   2
   1
   4

10. E
    C
    A
    D
    B

German General Level
Listening 2000

1. (a) No
   (b) 7.30

2. Buy stamps
   Go to a museum

3. Tomato soup
   Chicken
   Ice cream

4. 1st box (left hand box)

5. how many people live there
   the kind of house you live in

6. Market-(place)/Market (square)/
   Market car-park (Near the) market

7. (a) (Visit) castle/Palace/The (oldest) castle
   (b) Boat (trip)/Trip on lake/Go sailing/Go to the lake by boat/Go on the boats/Hiring a boat/Go on a boat trip to ... Lake (name of lake)

8. Comes from Switzerland/Bern/
   Lives in Switzerland/Born in Switzerland
   Is here with school (orchestra)/She plays in her school orchestra/School orchestra/School concert/School trip/Orchestra school
   Plays piano/keyboard

9. Tram (2nd box)
   On foot (4th box)

10. Cross at upper left box

11. Her room
    The weather

12. Has five rooms/five bedrooms/Has five-room bungalow
    Is in town (centre)/city/Near the town centre
    Has room/space (for you)/Has a room for you

13. Live in village/(called Dorf, Bergen, etc) in the mountains/hills/Beside the hills
    50 kilometres away/50 miles/50 kilometres from town centre

14. (a) (By) car/Father (will take you)/Drive in her father's car
    (b) Two hours

German General Level
Reading 2001

1. (a) Tick at "Train" (3rd box)
   (b) 16 (Marks)/16 (Pounds)
   (c) 85 (Marks)/85 (Pounds) (per day)

2. What are your interests?/What are you interested in?/What do you like doing?
   What is essential/important (for you) (in life)?
   Where have you worked?/What job(s) have you done?/What work experience have you had?/Have you had a job?/Have you worked?
   What are your favourite subject(s)?
   What do you like/enjoy at school?

3. *Doorman*
   (Long) coat
   either: Welcomes people/guest(s)/Greets guest(s)
   or: Opens car door(s)

   Hotel Housekeeper
   (White) blouse and (dark) skirt
   either: (Helps) when telephone out of action/broken/Fixes phone
   or: Gives toothbrush (if forgotten)/If you forget your toothbrush/No toothbrush/Sells toothbrush

   Restaurant Manager
   (Black) suit or (white) jacket
   either: Takes people to table(s)/Gives guests a table
   or: Gives menu

4. *Documentary* • 21.00
   Sports programme • 19.00
   Love story • 22.00
   Detective series • 20.00

5. Animals/pets
   (Too) difficult/Hard/Heavy-going
   Great/(Very) good/Cool/Brilliant/Fab
   Young people (in other countries)/
   Teenage life/Children/
   Teenagers (in the country)/Young men/Young women

6. Walking (3rd picture)
   Swimming (5th picture)
   Museum (2nd picture)

7. *Daniel*
   Saw film/Film is/was good/
   He liked the film/video
   Has the film/video/
   Because of the film/
   Has the film and thinks it's good

   Sarah
   Likes cats/Describes cats well/
   Cats are nice/She likes stories about cats/It's about cats

German General Level
Reading 2001 (cont.)

7. (cont.)

Lara
Got it from friend/Friend said it was good/Friend recommended it/
Friend introduced her to it/
Friend told her about it/
It was given to her

8. You should not
  either: Open window(s)
  or: Hide/Stay in room (under bed)/Stay under bed

  You should
  either: Close door(s)
  or: Dial 112/Phone fire brigade/Phone 999/Phone for help

9. (a) They/people/someone doesn't understand (you)/There's a misunderstanding/You don't understand (someone)/Not understanding
Someone doesn't listen (to you)/Someone doesn't hear you/They don't listen/You don't listen

  (b) **either**
  Write down what is annoying you/what you are thinking
  Throw (paper) away
  or
  Go to (best) friend/Talk to friend
  Ask them what they think
  you've done wrong/Tell them what's wrong/about it/
  Talk about your problems/
  Talk it through
  (Tell your (best) friend what is wrong = 2)

German General Level
Listening 2001

1. Half an hour/30 minutes

2. Tram
Underground
On foot

3. How do you spell your name?
Where do you live?
How long are you staying?

4. *History* • Positive
Biology • Positive

5. Tick at 2nd box

6. Baking/Making bread/Making rolls/Cooking bread
Shopping (for elderly/old folk)/
Old people shopping

7. Babysit/look after brother/Watch his brother/Brother is alone in the house/Has to go to his house with his brother/Brother is home/Has to be in for his brother/Has to play with brother/Has to feed his brother
Mum is visiting gran/grandparent in hospital/
Mum is at hospital with gran/
Mum and Gran are at hospital

8. (a) Caravan/Car/Camper/Camper-van/Mobile-home/Motor-home/Caravanette/
They are driving

  (b) Ticks at:
  Left hand box
  Lowest box

9. (Journey was) expensive/It was expensive
Too hot/Very hot/Terribly hot/So warm
Too warm/Very warm

10. 18.00 News
18.30 Wildlife
20.00 Sport

11. Go to music/guitar lesson/Go to music class/Watch daughter play guitar/
Go to music studio/Go to music school/Learn musical instrument/
Go with her/Go and do same as daughter
Have lunch/dinner/Have something to eat/Go for food/Have a meal/snack/Take her for lunch

12. Works/Helps in supermarket/at a checkout
Helps in house/Does housework/
Cleans the house/Tidies the house/Helps her mum/Works around the house

German General Level
Reading 2002

1. (a) Any **two** of:
  - Outskirts/Edge of town
  - (To the) west/(In the) West/On the West side/Westerly in the town
  - Next to/near stadium/At the stadium
  - 20 minutes from the station

  (b) • On foot/Walk

  (c) • Table tennis
  • Swimming

2. Ticks at:
  • You can wash in the rooms.
  • There are always children there.
  • The warden is nice.

3. Ticks at:
  • B
  • B

4. *Gertraud*
   - <u>Pen</u>-friend/<u>Letter</u> friend
   - Greece

   Markus
   - Home/In the house/indoors/In his house
   - Swim/Bathe/Bath in a pool

   Katerina
   - Mountains/Hills/Hilly area/In the hillsides
   - Walk/Hike/Ramble/Hike (and climb)/Hillwalk/Trekking/Go for a walk

5. *Heike*
   - ... wants to travel

   Martina
   - ... does not like it when people make fun of her

   Martina
   - ... prefers to be on her own when she is in a bad mood

6. (a) *Anna*
       Any **two** of:
       - Doesn't like it/Doesn't like the taste/Not a good taste/Not tasty
       - Thinks about animals/Involves death/killing/Dead animals/It's cruel to <u>kill animals</u>/She feels sorry for the animals/It's a shame about the animals/It was once an animal

       Joachim
       Any **two** of:
       - Not healthy
       - (Often) fatty/greasy
       - Makes you fat/You put on weight/Is fattening

   (b) *Pamela*
       - Father is butcher
       - Mother { makes / cooks meat <u>a lot</u>/(almost) always/<u>every day</u>/They have it <u>every day</u>/most days

7. (a) Ticks at:
       - Delivers newspapers
       - Helps out at home

   (b) - Knows where it is/Knows where it's going
       - (Always) gets it back/He pays/they pay him back

8. - <u>Teacher(s)</u> can <u>help</u>
   - Books/computers are there/They can use computers/School has all they need/He can do it on a computer/He can work on the computers
   - Has time for himself at home/When he gets home, the homework is done/Has rest of night free/No need to worry about homework once he's home

German General Level
Listening 2002

1. - Is at school/He has school/He has to go to school/He has something to do in school/He doesn't get out early enough/He has to be at school at two o'clock/He has to stay in school

2. (a) Tick at:
       - 3rd box (11.40)

   (b) Tick at:
       - 3rd box (three quarters of an hour)

3. - Is <u>15</u> minutes <u>late</u>/<u>Delayed</u> for <u>15</u> minutes/The bus will come at 11.55

4. Ticks at:
   - 3rd box (How was the journey?)
   - 4th box (When will you get here?)

5. - (Outside) post office/In front of/at/beside/near/next to/opposite the post-office/at the bus-stop at the post-office

6. (a) *horror films*
       - Likes them/Favourite type of film/They are good/Great/Enjoys/Brilliant/Likes "Hannibal"

   (b) *romantic films*
       - Doesn't like them/Don't interest her/They are rubbish/Are not her type/Doesn't like "Titanic"/They don't please her

7. Ticks at:
   - 2nd box (fishing)
   - 3rd box (rowing boat)
   - 4th box (walking)

8. - Cinema/Pictures/Watch a film
   - { Café/eat <u>ice cream</u> / Café<u>s</u>

9. - <u>Italian</u> restaurants/his { <u>fave</u> / <u>favourite</u> restaurant/An Italian place/An Italian

10. - Two meals (pizzas) for the price of one/2 for 1/Buy one, get one free/Two <u>people</u> for the price of one

11. Tick at:
    - 2nd box (book)

12. (a) *your bedroom* upper middle box
    (b) *bathroom* lower left box

13. Ticks at:
    - 3rd box (Have a shower)
    - 5th box (Have a sleep)
    - 6th box (Phone home)

German General Level
Listening 2002 (cont.)

14. (a) • Doctor/Surgery/Health Centre
    (b) • (Sore) throat/Throat infection

15. (a) Tick at:
    • 3rd box (Youth festival)
    (b) • He is playing in a band/drums/He is playing an instrument/See his band/His band is playing

German General Level
Reading 2003

1. • Prices are good/food (is good)/(Food is) great/good value/cheap/inexpensive
   • (Staff/boss/waiters are) friendly/(Chef and) staff/they are friendly/It is friendly/People are friendly/Service is friendly
   • (Nice/good) view

2. C
   E
   A
   B
   D

3. (Dog-sitting)
   • Feed(ing) the dog/The dog's food
   • Like animals/dogs/Fond of dogs

   (Bicycle courier)
   • Bring/take mail/letters/post/packages/parcels/documents (from one company to another)/Deliver packages
   • Phone manager/Contact manager/Call the manager/Speak to/ask manager (indication of talking to)

   (Babysitting)
   • Like children/Fond of babies
   • Ask neighbours/people in neighbourhood/Go round next door/By the neighbour(s)

4. • Eric
   • Ali
   • Carolin

5. B
   C
   A
   E
   D

6. (a) 3rd box (Interior designer)
   (b) 2nd box (Tour guide)

7. A Spends week-ends with (his) children/Plays with children at week-end/Goes out with children at week-ends
   B Breakfast with her husband/man
   C Walks in hills/mountains/Gets fresh air in mountains/Week-ends in mountains/Hill-walking/Wandering up hills
   D Climbs/runs/walks up stairs (to her office)/Runs up 287 steps

8. (a) Friday, 13.30
   (b) Meeting (his) group/Having lunch (with group) (from Leipzig)/Going out with group/Meeting with people
   (c) Dentist, taxi

9. • 2nd box (Near the airport)
   • 3rd box (Parking)
   • 6th box (Room with a shower)

German General Level
Listening 2003

1. 1st box (How long does the tour last?)
   4th box (Where does the bus leave from?)

2. 3rd box (Castle)
   5th box (Shopping centre)

3. • Lives nearby/close/near/near him/near me
   • Speaks good English/Is good at English/Has good English
   • Spent two years in Britain/UK

4. Any two from:
   • Weather (was terrible)
   • It rained (nearly every day)/It was wet
   • Caught a cold/Has a cold/Had a cold/Had flu
   (Weather was rainy = 2)

5. • 2nd box (Football match)
   • 3rd box (Boat trip on lake)
   • 5th box (Walk)

6. (a) Hospital
   (b) • Has (lots of) friends/Has made friends/Has new friends
       • Has (bought) a flat/house/Has found a nice place to live/Has her own flat/Has a place to live

7. (a) Every six weeks
   (b) Ferry/Boat/Ship (to/from Amsterdam)

8. (a) 2nd box
   (b) Eleven months

9. • Tuesday (evening)
   • 6.30/Half past six

10. (a) • Coast/Sea/Beach/Sea-side
    (b) • Swim
        • Walk/Go along the beach/Walk along the beach/Go along the pier

11. • 1st box (Homework)
    • 3rd box (Set table for breakfast)

German Credit Level
Reading 1999

1. (a) • Spend time in Israel (to learn language)
   (b) • Would have to join army
   (c) • Work in a fashion place/store/house/Become a model/Earn a lot of money <u>as a model</u>/Get into fashion (industry)
   (d) • If (face) was injured/in an accident it would be over/It would all change if she had an accident

2. (a) • Bridges sexes/generations/Appeals to people up to 50 years old
       • Will <u>remain</u> (when other fashions fade)
   (b) • Petrol costs money/Air/muscle power is free/cheap/Bike is cheaper
       • Bikes are friendlier to environment/Cars harm the atmosphere

3. (a) *Zemian*
       letter box
       • Needs mail <u>from</u> his <u>friend(s)</u>
       computer
       • Uses it for play/work/(if bored) he can use e-mail/Prevents boredom/Can write (e)-mail (to friends)
   (b) *Adeleke*
       cuddly toy
       • Would be <u>substitute</u> for friends/Wants a friend from home/He would have a friend/To keep him company/For when he's lonely
       chocolate
       • It makes you <u>happy</u>/joyous
   (c) *Martin*
       television
       • For relaxation
       sports ground
       • Keeping fit is important (to him)/Sport/health is <u>important</u>
   (d) *Arthur*
       books
       • Would have time to read/Books introduce him to (new) ideas
       canoe
       • To <u>escape</u> (from island)/to paddle <u>away</u>/Doesn't want to be stuck on island/To sail away

4. (a) • <u>Has</u> to clean bath/kitchen/hoover everywhere
       • She loses 5 Marks if she doesn't clean properly
       • Friends get more pocket money (but don't help as much)
   (b) Any **four** of:
       • Teenagers should get pocket money <u>without</u> working for it
       • Pocket money is important
       • Pocket money can teach how to handle money responsibly/teaches you the value of money/it teaches you to be responsible
       • Parents can expect children to help in house/Children should help in the house
       • But that shouldn't affect pocket money/Pocket money should not be influenced
   (c) • Speak to adults/parents <u>of friends</u>/neighbours/relatives (who are understanding/with whom you get on)
       • Find out from friends how much they get <u>and</u> what they pay for
       • (Think over arguments and) discuss things <u>calmly</u> with parents/Find a compromise with your parents

German Credit Level
Listening 1999

1. (a) • (To the) north/North Germany
   (b) • Has <u>aunt</u> there

2. (a) • <u>Friend's</u> <u>birthday</u> (party)/Go shopping
   (b) • <u>Buy</u> a <u>present</u>/Shop for a <u>present</u>

3. (a) • Go for/buy something to eat
   (b) • <u>Stay</u> with luggage/<u>Stay</u> in train/Look after the luggage

4. (a) • <u>Uncle</u> will take them
       • By <u>car</u>
   (b) Look round <u>old</u> <u>town</u>

5. • Go to their place at the beach/North Sea
   • Go to beach/Swim (in sea)/Paddle/Go to shore

6. (a) • Sunburn/sunstroke/heatstroke
   (b) • (Take to) doctor/Visit doctor/Get herself to doctor
       • (Get) treatment
         lotion   } (for sunburn)
         cream

7. • Visit Denmark/Go to Danish border
   • Drive along the (Baltic) coast/East Sea coast
   • Have (evening) meal/Go to a restaurant

German Credit Level
Listening 1999 (cont.)

8.
   - (Ulla/one) works in shopping centre/(big) store/shop/superstore
   - (Susanne/other friend) works with American firm/company/Works in export (department)

9. (a) EITHER
   - Quite far from town/Outside town/Is in an old building/old fashioned

   OR
   - The flat is nice (and is situated in an old district)

   (b)
   - Lots of trees/a pond/a lake/It's a quiet rural area (only if not used for (a))

10.
    - Can save money/sleep on train/It's cheaper
    - Have (whole) day to see town

11.
    - Get/borrow/hire bikes
    - Cycle back home/to Munich/München

German Credit Level
Reading 2000

1. (a) (Constantly/every day) reminding her of importance of exams/grades/doing well in exams/Pressure her into getting good results/Expect good marks/good "A" levels

   (b) Not bothered/Lost interest in school/not enjoying/no joy/no fun at school/Doesn't like/makes her less enthusiastic about school/no pleasure/Doesn't feel like going to school/Hates school

   Did no homework

   (c) Compares himself with others/wonders what they think of him/(in passive or active form)

   (outside cool)(inside) insecure/lacking confidence

   When he goes out he worries (about how he looks)

   (d) They react badly/Wonders how they will react when she brings boy home/round/They always react when she brings boy home/She's always afraid to take boys home

   They want him to be from same social class/group/from a good social group

   (e) Worries about making wrong choice(s)/about choosing wrong job/There are so many possibilities

   Worries about having to do so much/everything by himself/to care for himself/(idea of being independent)

   Taking decisions himself/Being an adult with a lot of responsibilities

2. (a) So she could get together/go out/with her friends
   or in the evening

   There was trouble because she went out so much

   Parents had ordered her not to go out/She would be forbidden to go out

   (b) That she had to get/to fetch/collect/something (important)

   (c) That she didn't have a boyfriend/male friend

   (d) Wanted to get to know him (better)

   She already had a boyfriend (if (c) is wrong)

   (e) Guitar cost (100 marks) more (than she thought)

   Lied about the cost of the guitar

   (f) So he could buy (new) clothes

   Plays in band, needs to look smart/good/stylish

3. (a) (They) (took him) to hospital after an accident/in an ambulance/
   A lot of people need our help/Gave him joy to help others/Helping people

   (b) Takes handicapped/disabled/wheelchair-bound (lady) to theatre (once a month)

   Talks about play/story/content (with her) (in interval/break)/
   Talking with her

   (c) He gets a lot from her/them

   His own problems are not so big/He sees his own problems in a different way

   Sees things differently

   (d) Interested in Japanese culture/Japanese culture is (quite) different from European/Likes Japanese culture/Fascinated by Japanese culture

   (Likes to be able to) do something others can't/Good feeling/She is the only one able to do it

   (e) Tolerance of others/understanding (for) (of) others/people

   Is learning a lot about young people (in Japan)/school in Japan

German Credit Level
Listening 2000

1. When did you leave/start from home?/When did you leave Scotland?/When did you get out of the house?

   Did you spend the night in Munich?/Did you stay in Munich?/Did you stop over in Munich?

2. Have to wait for (next) train/More guests(s) (are arriving in ten minutes)/Waiting for guests to get off the train/Have to wait for someone else/More guests are arriving for lessons/Have to wait for guests' train

3. (a) Fill in form/Check in/Sign in/Register/Give her your details/Fill in sheet

   (b) Single room/Room has one bed/Have your own room
   Non-smoking
   Second floor

4. (a) (breakfast) Next door/In another building/In the main building/In the building opposite/In the building on the right

   (b) (lunch) Collect (from cook) (from kitchen)/(It's a) packed lunch

   (c) (evening meal) Traditional/Austrian/Special from Austria/Food from Austria

5. (a) Meeting in cellar/Trying out/on the equipment/
   Going to cellar/basement/
   Get boots and skis

   (b) Thick/heavy socks/Big socks/Warm socks/Ski socks
   Photo (for ski pass)/Photo (for identity)/Photo and passport

6. (a) Nice/polite/friendly (to him)/
   Gets on well with them/Treat him with respect

   (b) Learn (to ski) (more) quickly/Learn better Learn easier/Learn to ski faster/Very keen/Very eager/Ski fast(er)

7. (a) See sights/Tour round town/
   Visit city/See old town

   (b) Go shopping (in town centre)/Go to shopping-centre/Go to buy things/Go shopping and have lunch/Do (the) shopping/window-shopping/Buy presents/souvenirs

8. Lives in city/town/Finds (all) town(s)/city centre(s) boring
   Would rather go hiking/for a walk/be in countryside/go into country/stay in the country(side)/Go on trip to countryside

9. Lost a boy (in mountains)/Lost a child/young person/15-year old got lost
   Searched for hour(s)/Couldn't find him/Sent out search-party/Someone went to look for him/Took hour(s) to find him (idea of search must be present)
   He turned up after (four) hours

10. Shivering (with anxiety)/fear/Shaking/In shock/Was very scared/Was afraid/Panicking/Worried/Anxious to get home/Not calm/Shivering/shaken Could barely walk/Couldn't walk/Couldn't move/Could hardly stand/Had to sit down/Had to carry him

11. (a) (Scotland) Not/never far from sea/Lots of seaside/The sea

    (b) (Austria) Snow lasts long(er)/Mountains are high/Always snow in mountains/Snow all year round

German Credit Level Reading 2001

1. (a) Mother heard they were looking for actor(s)/actress(es)/people/
   Mother heard about the part/it
   (Mother) sent photos/CV/curriculum/portfolio
   (Mother) took photos of her and sent them off/(Mother) handed in photos/took and gave them photos

   (b) When friend(s) are round .../When she plays with her friend(s) .../When friend(s) come to stay ...
   They dress up
   They act/They play theatre/They put on shows

   (c) Parents stayed with her (in hotel)/Mum and Dad came along with her/She got to see her parents in hotel/Parents stayed in the same hotel/Close to her parents
   People explained what she had to do/told her what to do
   People/the crew helped her to do what she had to do

   (d) Could have continued (for weeks)/Enjoyed the experience/It was a good experience/She wants filming to continue

   (e) Imagined her dog was dead/Told herself her dog was going to die/Kept remembering her dog was going to die/Someone told her the dog was dead
   Kept thinking "Be serious!"

2. (a) *Ricky*
   Paints (scenes from Africa)
   Kristin
   Makes dresses/clothes/Designs clothes
   Heike
   Goes to café/Meets/talks with friends/Talks about God/world

   (b) *Ricky*
   Tolerance of others/People are tolerant
   Kristin
   Having freedom/learning to be independent/stand on their own feet
   Heike
   (Doing something for) environment/Cares for the environment/Recycling

German Credit Level
Reading 2001 (cont.)

2. (cont.)

(c) *Ricky*
Travel (world)

Kristin
Work with <u>poor</u>/Work in <u>Third World</u>/Help in <u>Third World</u>/Help the poor

Heike
Be a Green politician/Join the <u>Greens</u>/<u>Green</u> politics

3. (a) Has { taken part/<u>raced</u> in Australia and America/qualified for races in Australia <u>and</u> America }

(Had a) Good time(s)/Is fast/Even with good times

Is <u>taking part</u> in { Olympics / Paralympics }

<u>Compete</u> in the Paralympics/He will be at the Paralympics

(b) They pushed him (up hill)/They pushed him (in his wheelchair)/They helped him <u>up a mountain</u>/<u>up a hill</u>

<u>They</u> tried out wheelchair/He let them try out his wheelchair

(c) Puts football shoes/boots on his hands/Plays with his hand(s)/They play with their hands

Plays in goal(s)

(d) Homework/Home exercises

German Credit Level
Listening 2001

1. No (underground) station <u>at airport</u>/No (underground) station (near) <u>here</u>
   Can take bus (to underground)/<u>mini</u>bus/(chartered) bus/(airport) bus
   (Station) is <u>five minutes</u> (walk) away

2. <u>Breakfast</u> is at 07.30/<u>Breakfast</u> is at a different time/<u>Breakfast</u> is no longer at 7/<u>Breakfast</u> is from 7.30
   Washing (machines) is three <u>Marks</u>/DM/3M (Special) wash is DM3/Washing is now a different price/<u>One</u> pound/Washing clothes costs 3 marks

3. *Matthias*
   Is studying <u>medicine</u>/Is going to study medicine

   Steffi
   University is good/Universities are good/Heard university is better/good/the education is good

   Any **two** from three:
   Visiting Matthias/Is here to see Matthias (again)/Back to visit friends

3. (cont.)
<u>Met</u> him last summer/in Austria/<u>Met</u> him <u>last</u> year/<u>Met</u> him in summer/Knows him from last summer

Is on holiday

4. <u>Eat</u> in <u>pub/student café/students' union/student place/student restaurant</u>/Students' club
   (Go to) (art) gallery/<u>art</u> museum/art festival/art exhibition

5. By underground/tube/subway/metro

6. (a) Any **one** of two:
   Go to office/Start off in the office/Report to reception/Report to him
   Wear jeans <u>and</u> T-shirt/Bring jeans <u>and</u> T-shirt (**or** trousers)

   (b) Wellingtons/<u>working</u> clothes/overalls/boots/footwear/protective clothing/special clothing/clothes to wear on top/boiler suit/dungarees

7. Any **two** of:
   Do work of absent worker/A worker is ill
   Working in monkey-house
   Cleaning out (cages)/Cleaning out the animals/Clean out the monkeys (changing bedding)
   Feeding (animals)

8. (a) School trip/group (from Manchester/England)/School class/Group from Manchester/People from England/Tourists from England

   (b) You could give tour in English/You can speak English with them
   You can speak with them
   (If "from Manchester/from England" is mentioned in the first point)/You can translate for them

9. Lunch is 12.30–13.30/Lunch is at 12.30
   Canteen is opposite elephants/at/near/across from/beside/past/
   It (ie lunch) is opposite . . .
   <u>Fish</u> is good/<u>Fish</u>-pie is good/<u>Fish</u>-suppers are good

10. Meet people from different places/
    You can come from all over the world
    (Lots of) culture/museums/theatre/music (any <u>two</u> of)
    (Lots of) green spaces/parks/woods/
    Can do walks/The city is green/lots of greenery

11. Any **two** of:
    Found a flat/somewhere to live/Has a flat/Has found a house/Bought a flat
    <u>10 minutes</u> from <u>university</u>
    Big/bright room(s)/bedroom(s)
    Sharing with (two) <u>boys</u>/men
    Sharing with <u>two</u> people/
    Sharing with people from North Germany